GRAIL

BECOMING LIGHT – LIVING LOVE

A COLLECTION OF WRITINGS

Published 2001
Edward Gaskell Publishers
6 Grenville Street
Bideford
Devon
EX39 2EA

First Published 2001

isbn 1-898546-44-4

GRAIL
Becoming Light — Living Love
A collection of Writings

Use of the images by Nanette Crist Johnson does not necessarily imply an endorsement by the artist of the ideas represented in this publication.

Cover image of Archangel Melchizedek © 1985-2002 AD Nanette Crist Johnson

Printed and Bound by
Lazarus Press
Unit 7 Caddsdown Business Park
Bideford
Devon
EX39 3DX

THE TEMPLE OF LOVE AND LIGHT

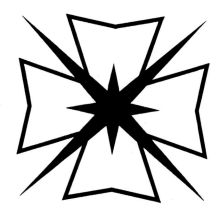

Profits from the sale of this book will go to The Trinity Foundation, which is the caretaker for the manifestation of the **Temple of Love and Light**. This architectural marvel of a pyramidal structure will have a base of nearly 500 feet per side and an external height of approximately 450 feet. The interior structure of the Temple will comprise seven levels, symbolically representing seven steps to human spiritual development.*

The Trinity Foundation is a non-profit research, development and educational organization dedicated to the study of human spirituality and enlightenment. Its primary purposes are

1. to research the universal concepts that underlie the beliefs of people of all cultures and religions, focusing on unity rather than divisions resulting from dogma;

2. to develop and provide educational programs that reflect this unity and assist individuals to evolve spiritually; and

3. to build a structure called the **Temple of Love and Light** as a forum for teaching and learning, as well as a focal point for all that The Trinity Foundation represents. Individuals world-wide may share diverse viewpoints regarding spirituality and the common threads uniting spiritual paths among humankind.

The Foundation's intent is to leave a legacy contributing to a more harmonious world, where people who have developed attributes of honesty, integrity, forgiveness, non-judgment, truthfulness, courage, willingness to face fears, kindness, generosity, and trust, to name only a few, will work together in pursuit of common goals -- in other words, Unity and Oneness for All.

*The Foundation's website may be visited at www.trinityfoundation.com

The Grail Cup

CONTENTS

PART ONE
IN SEARCH OF THE HOLY GRAIL

PART TWO
ENERGY WORK IN ENGLAND

PART THREE
CODES IN NEW JERUSALEM

PART FOUR
THE SPIRIT OF AUSTRALIA

PART FIVE
SANCTUARY OF THE DIVINE MOTHER

FOREWORD

The writings of this Journal have come into being at the request of Archangel Metatron, who shortly after our return home from the Journey "In Search of the Holy Grail" in France delivered the following request:

> All the undertakings of your group must be recorded in chronological order, detailing individuals' previous incarnational connections, detailing the experiences of your Journey and Quest in France and the continuation of this mission here.*

The seeds sown by Archangel Metatron in January 1998 soon sprouted. They have grown over the months, nurtured with much love and enthusiasm with contributions from many members of the group, and eventually have ripened and matured into the fruits of this colourful Journal.

With contributions from

Sandy, Irene, Felicity and Gisela	–	England
Kate, Lynne and Ruth	–	America
Lesley and Jill	–	Australia

– compiled by Gisela –

*Channelled by Edwin Courtenay, London, 31.1.1998.

© Armando de Melo

INTRODUCTION

THE DREAM OF CAMELOT
– Reawakening the Vision of King Arthur –

Once upon a time there was a great King; his name was Arthur. He lived in England in **Camelot Castle.**

King Arthur together with Merlin brought the dream of **Camelot** to the land -- a vision of unity, equality, truth, courage, integrity and honour -- a dream of a higher world forming for the children of Earth.

However, it was the time of the Dark Ages and their hopes and dreams came crashing down and were laid dormant. Merlin fell asleep and has been resting in his crystal cave ever since.

Over one thousand and four hundred years later there incarnated on Earth the Children of Light to assist in the Divine Plan -- to create **Camelot** once again for the world.

They have been full of courage, displaying discipline and dedication. They have to be pure of heart and clear of mind, mastering unconditional love and forgiveness. They have been travelling across the planet restoring balance and harmony on Earth, balancing Earth's electromagnetic fields, receiving Codes and carrying these for the world. They have worked with the elemental kingdom to bring greater blessings to Earth, and made contact with indigenous people to reclaim ancient wisdom.

Many gifts have been received by the Children of Light on these challenging Journeys: experiencing new levels of consciousness, raising their energy fields to a higher vibration, being offered the opportunity to confront and release old karma, returning home transformed and renewed.

They witnessed a Portal Opening during one of their Journeys and the foundation was laid for the next phase of the collective mission. The memory of **Camelot** was being reawakened within. All were being prepared to enter the Kingdom of the City of Light.

They were taken to England, for here the Codes for the **Camelot** energy were being held. The purpose of this Journey was to reawaken Merlin or the magic within -- to search for the knowledge and wisdom necessary to feed the vision of tomorrow.

The sun began to shine upon the land as an accelerated shift of consciousness was created within the minds of humanity -- for the City of Light **Camelot** truly is the Light within the mind. The clarity of the vision and the remembrance of ancient wisdom could now begin to rise in consciousness around the land.

Next followed the mission to capture the Holy Grail and return it to **Camelot** so the dream for creating the Cities of Light may become realized on Earth. Thus began the Journey "In Search of the Holy Grail". The foundation was laid for bringing **Camelot**, the City of Light, into the Seventh Golden Age.

It is a mission that is living on -- now as an Inner Journey -- a Journey of the soul. Living the truths, the Grail mysteries are lived on, paving the way to our enlightenment.*

The writings of this Journal are dedicated to the reader
as an invitation to embark, through sharing the Grail Journey,
on the deepening of his or her personal Journey of self-discovery --
to reach into the inner chambers of the heart
in search for the mysteries of the Grail --
an invitation to follow the Holy Spirit Dove,
drinking from the Cup of Divine Light,
filling the heart with love.
May joy accompany the reader on this Journey.

*Retold from Master Kuthumi's Messages
  Status Report Concerning the Portal Opening North of Kiev, Majestic Raise, Jan/Feb/March 1996.
  The Merlin Within Us Now Awakens, Majestic Raise, Oct/Nov/Dec 1996.
  Transmissions received by Dr. Norma Milanovich, Albuquerque, NM, 1996.
  Copyright at Athena Leadership Center.

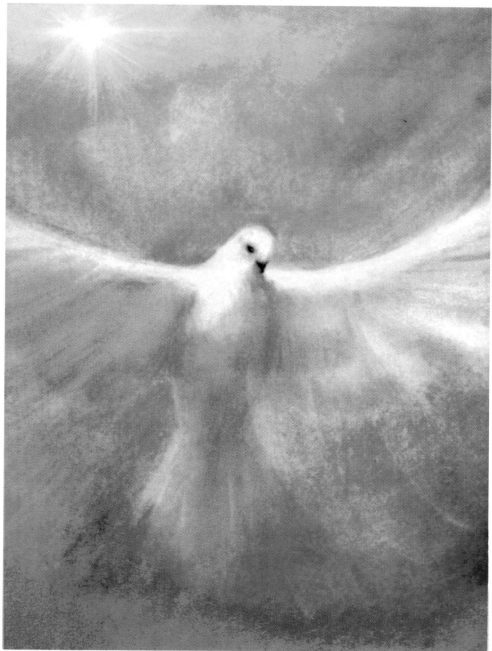

The Holy Spirit Dove

PART ONE

IN SEARCH OF THE HOLY GRAIL

Drawn together by their karmic connections, 48 Knights of Old travelled through France in search of higher truths -- pursuing spiritual growth on their own path to enlightenment, and in service to humanity.

A CALL GOES OUT FOR A JOURNEY TO FRANCE

© 1985-2002 AD Nanette Crist Johnson   The Grail Knight

In the Summer of 1997 a call went out from Ascended Master Kuthumi for 48 Knights of Old to gather and undertake a Journey to France "In Search of the Holy Grail" under the leadership of Dr. Norma Milanovich, who had by then conducted 17 Journeys around the world under the guidance of the Spiritual Hierarchy.   These Journeys were undertaken to bring to the Earth enlightenment and evolution, to assist in bringing the Seventh Golden Age to Earth.[1]

[1]*Sacred Journey to Atlantis* by Dr. Norma Milanovich and Jean Meltesen.
 Athena Publishing, Albuquerque, NM 87109-1574, 1992.

Norma, through her 'direct link' with Master Kuthumi, not only provided us before and during the Journey with all necessary instructions, but led us on the Journey with great skill. Her devotion to the plan and her selfless service to the Divine is an inspiration to us all. Thank you, Norma.

Master Kuthumi came to us dressed as a Knight standing behind the Sword of Excalibur as he delivered his Coded Message:

There shall be one focus on this Journey and that is to capture the Holy Grail and return it to **Camelot** *so the dream for creating the Cities of Light may become realized on Earth....* This Journey represents the last battle that must be won for the Most Radiant One, before the cosmic clocks tick to a new time.

There are a total of 48 Knights of Old who presently live in embodiment on Earth who will understand what this message means. It is to those souls whom I speak, for it was they who took oaths of completion, centuries ago, to guard the secrets of the Grail until the time was right to bring this wisdom forth for the world.

THE TIME IS NOW and the cosmic clocks tick to the rhythm of the New Awakening, Dear Sisters and Brothers of the Grail. Stretch and yawn as you are being called to move into a new consciousness and prepare to receive the information that will change the heart and mind of the world.

There are three Keys that must be delivered to the Knights to whom I speak, that will arouse the spirit within. These three Keys are:

1. The Light from the dawn touches the castle at the precise moment when Venus is aligned with the higher wisdom of the heart.

2. The heart holds seven Codes that must be released at Point Zero on the Ile de la Cité, Notre Dame Cathedral, St. Michel's Mount, Carnac, Chartres Cathedral, Rennes-le-Chateau and Montségur. Prepare to move into battle and position yourselves with the Archangels of Power to deliver these Codes to the world.

3. The archetype and oversoul of Joan of Arc holds the portal open for only 14 days while the siege endures. Align with the spirit of Oneness and love and Ye shall be delivered from harm's way.

In the darkness of Winter and the Light of day shall the Knights travel to the land of antiquities and dreams. This Journey will not be as easy as the other Journeys in the past, especially endured during the darkness of Winter, and the Knights who step forth and commit to raising the Grail into Shamballa know this.

Do you, today, have the courage and discipline it will take to complete this mission, that you had when you took your oaths of honour? If so, then step onto the platform of Light and prepare to journey with El Morya and myself into the land of secrets and dreams. We, with the assistance of Joan of Arc, will guide your footsteps through the labyrinths that lead to the Grail. Ye shall discover the mosaic that is and always has been within you and Ye shall also be liberated in the Light of the Most High as you complete your duty with honour and glory.

Let the battles begin.

Kodoish, Kodoish, Kodoish Adonai Tsebayoth.

I AM Kuthumi.[2]

[2]*Kuthumi Sends a Coded Message to 48 Knights of Old Who Are Destined to Discover the Secrets of the Holy Grail.*
Transmission received by Dr. Norma Milanovich, Albuquerque, NM, 1997.
Copyright at Athena Leadership Center.

THE SPIRITUAL HISTORY OF THE HOLY GRAIL
- Message from Master Kuthumi -

© Armando de Melo

In preparation for the Journey "In Search of the Holy Grail" Edwin Courtenay, a gifted spiritual teacher here in England, channelled Master Kuthumi and provided us with a Message on the "Spiritual History of the Holy Grail".

Master Kuthumi started by stating that the information given would be vital to unlocking not only some of the secrets and mysteries of the Grail's power, but also the energies and dimensional doorways, windows and portals that would allow us to access and enter into the fullness of the Grail force.

He delivered the following discourse:

It is important to understand the nature of the Holy Grail, what it truly is, what it represents and the part that it has to play in the unfoldment of mankind's evolution.

The Grail is a symbolic archetypal energy. It is connected to the feminine force of the Divine. It is connected to grace and flow, vision and receptivity, healing, intuition, psychicism, dreams. It is connected to wisdom and to attuning to the nurturing source-energy of the Divine, to the feminine part of our own nature, which is closest to and connected with the abundant free-flowing mother-divine energy of the universe.

The Holy Grail existed in ancient times as an archetypal symbolic form that was associated with the divine nurturing energy of the Archangel Melchizedek. Melchizedek is the Archangel who is responsible for passing on to his angelic brethren the energy of the Divine that is needed by the angelic hierarchies in order that they may sustain their existence and utilize the power to perform the will of God.

In time, when mankind was created, it was decided and seen that the Grail's energy needed to be passed on to humanity, that they needed to be enabled to attune themselves to the source's energy through this archetypal image and symbol, that they now needed to be awoken to their own inner feminine energy and power in order that they may more closely recognize their own divinity and utilize it for the greater good of their species.

The Grail's energy, therefore, was projected down the vibrational scale of the angelic hierarchy and given in a fashion to the Archangel Gabriel. The Archangel Gabriel's Holy Grail, therefore, is a vibrational down-scaled, down-loaded version of the Holy Grail that is still possessed on a more cosmic level by the Archangel Melchizedek. The Archangel Gabriel utilized the energies of this Holy Grail, of this symbol, of this force, to awaken and enlighten mankind to their own inherent feminine energy, qualities and characteristics.

When Lemuria came to an end and Atlantis was risen, it was recognized that individuals were required in order to anchor the seven cosmic archetypal energies upon the Earth that were needed by mankind in order to grow and evolve.

These energies were represented by elemental archangels and the forces that they governed over:

the powers of earth, wisdom and growth,
the powers of air, communication and healing,
the powers of fire, transformation, passion and protection,
the powers of water, dream, intuition, psychicism,
the powers of spirit, knowing, enlightenment, truth,
the power of love, and
the powers of change and transformation;

represented by the Archangels Uriel, Raphael, Michael, Gabriel, Azrael, Hanael and Zamuel.

Seven royal families were constructed in Atlantis. And each of the royal families had the duties of maintaining and anchoring the vibrational force of these cosmic archetypal elements onto the Earth. Symbols of their powers were created and the archangels themselves filled these symbols with force and Light. The original physical Holy Grail was filled with energy from the ethereal Holy Grail in the possession of the Archangel Gabriel. It was kept and maintained by the royal families of Atlantis and its energy and power utilized to maintain the vibration of love, dreams, intuition and the feminine force of the emotion on the Earth.

At the time of the great destruction the royal families had fallen into disarray. They were no longer living in harmony, but, reflecting the nature of the world around them, they existed in a constant skirmish, squabbling, fighting, seeking supremacy and power over the other. The archangels had long since abandoned them, knowing now that it was impossible to provide them with any form of guidance that they were willing to listen to, and to a large extent they had withdrawn their energetic support, leaving these symbols and tools of power as void, useless objects, carrying no Light, no strength, no divinity.

The majority of these original hallows were destroyed in the great destruction, but throughout history they would be reconstructed again and again. Their images would be drawn from the Akashic Records as etheric blue-prints and they would be manufactured and reshaped and remade.

Before Jesus was born a great deal of prophets and seers and visionaries foresaw the nature and importance of his coming. Jesus would bring a new age to the world, shifting the focus from the matriarchal energy to the patriarchal force as was ordained and willed by the Divine.

But the energy and knowledge that Jesus was to bring to mankind was not to be devoid of the feminine energy, but was to simply contain it and carry it in a different dynamic, in a different balance, in a different fashion and form, and, therefore, the guidance was given by the angels to mankind again to reshape the Holy Grail in order that it might be given to the boy-child Jesus, that he would keep it and utilize its power at a later date when it was needed and necessary.

A stone fell to Earth, a meteorite, a large piece of the powerful energy-stone known as Moldavite, and it was from this glassy ore that the Grail was created, was forged.

The Grail was given to the boy-child Jesus by one of the three Magi at a very early stage in Jesus's childhood, and the Grail was kept and utilized from time to time. But it was only towards the end of Jesus's life that he acknowledged the importance of the Grail and its power and utilized it in ceremony and ritual in order to imbue it with a certain aspect of his consciousness, the Christ consciousness and the divine frequency and energy of the Light under which he operated at that time.

Strict instructions were given to his uncle Joseph of Arimathea to collect blood in the chalice. The blood was to mix with the existing water that was in the chalice that was utilized at the last Supper, blood and holy water joining together to form a powerful symbol of purity and sacrifice.

Joseph of Arimathea was guided to take the Holy Grail, the chalice, with him to England, where he was guided to begin to set down the structure of the spiritual truth as taught by Jesus at that time. He knew that the age of the matriarchal was over, and so too did the High Priestesses of Britain.

Joseph was instructed that at a later time the Holy Grail, which in the beginning was to be planted in Glastonbury, would merge with another manifestation of the Grail's energy, which was called the cauldron of Cerridwen. The cauldron of Cerridwen was the matriarchal equivalent of the patriarchal Holy Grail. It was a pagan symbol for the cosmic womb, but it carried inside it masculine elements of creativity, motivational spark and the beginning of life. When the time was right, a long time after Joseph's death, the Holy Grail would be taken to the Island of Glass in Glastonbury, and it would be merged with the cauldron of Cerridwen in order that the two energies might become balanced. When this indeed occurred both combined energies entered into the ether, where they have remained since, returning from time to time to this plane in order to provide mankind with their benefit, with their power, with their strength.

Indeed, it was when Arthur, through his folly, had jeopardized the life-force of England itself, that the Holy Grail appeared to him in order to restore to both him and the land the balanced energy of the matriarchal and patriarchal forces that was needed and required in order to allow England to continue to grow and evolve.

Before the Grail was merged with the cauldron of Cerridwen it resided for some time in Glastonbury. It was known to be there, protected by powerful angelic forces, powerful magic that defied anyone's true understanding, that was considered to be miraculous.

In love and peace, in trust we bid you farewell[3].

[3]Channelled by Edwin Courtenay, London, 3.9.1997.

OUR TRAINING PROGRAMME

Several months before the start of the Journey the Knights, who guarded the secrets of the Grail, were initiated into a training programme for their mission, as outlined by Master Kuthumi:

Isis watches over the moon at night and aligns Venus with the Temple of the New Dawn. The radiance from her soul touches all who collectively gather on the eve of the Winter Solstice which will open the portal of understanding regarding the secrets of the Grail.

- Each of the 48 Knights who align with this energy will open higher wheels of evolution within their own consciousness and begin to sing the tales of old.

- The Third Eyes of the spiritually elite will record new symbols and the secrets of the Holy Grail will be revealed and recorded in the days and years to come.

*All in Heaven and on Earth shall rejoice for the foundation will be complete for bringing **Camelot**, the City of Light, into the Seventh Golden Age.*

Discipline was needed for us to move through the labyrinths of the mind. We were asked to walk each day in silence and contemplation.

Three Archangels of Power positioned themselves around those who had committed to complete this Journey and formed, aligned with the trinity of Master El Morya, Joan of Arc and Master Kuthumi, a protective shield around each member who was preparing for battle. Michael, Raphael and Tzadkiel were assisting with the training to prepare the Knights' minds and hearts for a successful completion of this mission.

Our training consisted of the following daily meditation over many weeks:

Hold all consciousness intact
and focus all power within the Third Eye.

Visualize a pinpoint of Light in the Third Eye
and create one shape with this Light.

Hold this symbol of power within
for a period of eight minutes each day.

Simultaneously, hold an image of golden Light
radiating in the heart

and bring Excalibur to the point of stillness
that touches the rod of power within.[4]

In addition, we had to draw the symbol of power we were receiving. This was to be shared with the others at Mont-St-Michel.

We were preparing ourselves for the adventure of the century. This routine would prepare each Knight's soul to remember and release the secrets of the Grail and to touch the hand of Isis.

© Armando de Melo

KARMIC CONNECTIONS
- Message from Master Kuthumi -

We had all expected that we had met before in previous lifetimes, but little did we know how strict the rules for selection were for us to qualify for the Mission. During the Journey Master Kuthumi revealed the selection procedure to us.

A High Council Meeting was held between what is called the 11th and 12th century (after the Templars -- who carried the secrets of the Grail Mysteries, were suppressed), to select 48 souls, residing on the etheric, who would agree to serve as vessels to hold these secrets in their souls until the time was right to release them. These 48 souls had not yet been touched by the Black Magicians and still held the golden thread in their souls' lineage that connected them to the Temple of the Grail in the Great Central Sun. While there were more than 48 to choose from, the Council knew that only 48 were needed to complete the mission. The Knights were selected using the following criteria.

1. Each soul had to have been an Atlantian High Priest or Priestess in good standing with the Karmic Board.
2. Each soul had to have been an Essene and participated in creating the Dead Sea Scrolls.
3. Each soul had to have been in the Temple of Isis and trained in Egypt's Mystery Schools.
4. Each soul had to have been a Cathar and died for the truths, thus exhibiting courage, honour and integrity to the end.
5. Each soul had to have been a Knight Templar who actually touched both the Grail and the Ark of the Covenant and is ready to prepare to move both on Earth to the position of human consumption.
6. Each soul had to have been in **Camelot** and held a responsible position for creating the dream for the world.
7. Each soul had to agree to come to Earth at this time to join in service to complete the mission to unlock the pathway to the Temple of the Grail in the Great Central Sun.

The 48 who were finally selected were ultimately selected because of their commitment to purify and stand in higher truths to assure the success of this collective mission.[5]

[5]*France Journey, Fifth Message Received Enroute.*
Transmission received by Dr. Norma Milanovich, Albuquerque, NM, 1997.
Copyright at Athena Leadership Center.

THE ARK OF THE COVENANT
- Message from Lady Portia -

Considering the connectedness of the Ark of the Covenant and the Holy Grail the Spiritual Hierarchy provided us with a discourse on the Ark of the Covenant, which was graciously given by Lady Portia, who introduced herself as follows:

I am Lady Portia, Lady of Shamballa, female Ascended Master.

As with the Holy Grail, the Ark of the Covenant exists no longer in the physical form, but has long since passed into the etheric plane. It can also be found microcosmically within ourselves.

The Ark of the Covenant was said in the beginning to contain within it the Tablets of Moses, which bore the Commandments of God. This is not true.

The ten Commandments that are recorded in the Bible are a fallacy -- something that has been created by mankind in order to control and manipulate those who would worship a patriarchal God.

The Commandments were spiritual Laws and Truths. These Laws and Truths were given by the Divine to mankind in order that they might work with them, so that they could play their part as co-creators of their world, working in accordance with the Universal Laws that would aid them in the manifestation and transformation of themselves and the environment that surrounded them.

The Ark of the Covenant was that which contained these Universal Laws. It was a storehouse for their manifestation and power. It was a receptacle in which this wisdom was held.

The Ark of the Covenant now exists guarded over by the high archangelic beings. It resides between the Archangel Melchizedek and the Archangel Metatron and is held in a form of energetic stasis until the day when it will be appropriate for it to be returned to mankind and placed back into their overall consciousness.

The Ark itself was raised in vibrationary status so that it could be released from the physical bondage of this Earth plane and taken into the higher spiritual zones.

The Ark itself was created through the direction of God by God's disciples and servants. It was created utilizing certain high vibrational metals and stones in order that the spiritual wisdom, which was, of course, a conscious Light, could be sufficiently contained within them.

The spiritual Laws were not set in stone, but were created and placed within an enlightened tome, a form of Bible or spiritual Holy Book. The miracle was that the Bible itself was self-fulfilling: it would re-write itself and new sections would miraculously and marvellously appear. As and when certain spiritual Laws became appropriate for mankind to see and become aware of, these Laws would appear inside of this great book of wisdom, with a great deal of oratory written as to how the Laws could be utilized in the re-creation of the Earth.

These Laws were written in this tome, in this tablet of wisdom, by the Archangel Ezekiel, who is the divine scribe.

When it was decided that these Laws were no longer safe upon the Earth, the Ark was ascended and translated into vibrational energy patterns that are now stored between these two archangelic beings.

The Ark of the Covenant exists inside ourselves as our capacity and potential to access this wisdom and this truth. Although we believe ourselves at this moment in time to be aware of spiritual Laws, there are others that we do not know presently, which will return to our consciousness as and when we are ready and able to assimilate and digest them. At this time we will find a way inside ourselves to contact and attune ourselves to the energy frequency that is at this moment the Ark of the Covenant and the tome of wisdom, the tablets of spiritual truth, that are contained within it. We will then bring forward this truth and live by it, transforming ourselves and the world accordingly with these spiritual Laws and with these Laws of Light.

In truth and trust and joy we leave you with our love
and take our leave.[6]

[6]Channelled by Edwin Courtenay, London, 29.7.1998.

London ■

ENGLISH CHANNEL

Dunkerque

Calais

Lille

BELGIUM

● <u>Rouen</u>

Caen ●

<u>Mt-St-Michel</u>

Paris
■

Reims ●

Verdun

<u>Carnac</u> ● Rennes

<u>Chartres</u>

Nantes ●

● Tours   ● Orléans

● Bourges

● Poitiers

● Dijon

Besançon ●

● La Rochelle

F R A N C E

SWITZERLAND

● Clermont-
Ferrand

● Bordeaux

● Lyon

● Cahors

Grenoble ●

ITALY

Lourdes ●

PYRÉNÉES

Toulouse ●

Carcassonne ●

Montségur <u>Rennes-
le -Chateau</u>

● Nîmes

Avignon ●

SPAIN

ANDORRA

● Perpignan

Marseille ●

MEDITERRANEAN   SEA

COMING TOGETHER AGAIN
- A Time for Guidance and Our Initial Ceremony -

Photo by Antonio Genco

And so we came together again. On the night of Wednesday, December 10, 1997, we met as a group in Paris for discussions, guidance and our opening ceremony.

The ceremony was based on the information given by Master Kuthumi, which was that Isis was to place a seven-pointed star within each heart on the first night of the Journey. This symbol of power was to strengthen our hearts for battle.

We were advised to include the Pentagram in our ritual and received the explanation that this ancient symbol of the Divine represents the Adam Kadmon and its full development on Earth in that it incorporates earth, fire, water, air and Spirit -- the Goddess of the soul.[7]

[7]See discourse *The Adam Kadmon* p.20.

Our entire Journey through France was to be guided by Master Kuthumi, Master El Morya and Joan of Arc, the "Trinity of the Grail".

Master Kuthumi assured us of the following assistance:

> We, the Trinity of the Grail, ...combine the energies in our hearts and beam three strands of golden Light from the Temple of the Grail in the Great Central Sun to each participant who has agreed to make this Journey successful. These three strands of Light will infuse within the souls of the members the Codes to release the mysteries of the Grail for the world.
>
> For this Journey, we, the Trinity of the Flame, give unto the group the symbol of the Dove... The dove shall be the symbol of power and will show the group the way. Watch for it and prepare to have it assist you, especially out of the mazes and the labyrinths of your minds.
>
> Joan of Arc holds the Keys for the magic to emerge and she is prepared to ride ahead of the group to assure that the chambers of the Most High are ready to receive the group's collective oversoul. At each sacred site, she will sound Gabriel's trumpet and prepare the site with the frequency that will raise the group's Light vibrations to the note of "A". Standing, then, in the Light of the Great Central Sun, she will hold the torch that will light each site and ignite the Codes that are destined to be released.

We were informed that the key to a successful Journey in France would be each member's ability to clearly hear and transmit information, following inner guidance, and that each of the 48 Knights had worked for years to assure that their clarity and purity of heart were intact.

We were instructed to meditate as a group for a period of 30 minutes daily.

On the Journey each member's soul had to connect to the "Ninth Dimension" so that the Grail mysteries held within the hearts and souls could be released. The section of the "Ninth Dimension" that the group had to enter is a parsec of the universe that had not been explored by humans since the days when Jesus walked the face of the Earth. This was to be done by holding the frequency of our perfect sound during the day by smiling often, staying calm at all times and reciting three decrees that would hold one's consciousness on the Grail at all times and align the Heart Chakra with Venus.

The decrees to recite were:

> Through the Divine Higher Presence of God, I decree that I am perfectly calm and see the illusions that contribute to unconsciousness all around me. I now detach from the illusions.

> Through the Divine Higher Presence of God, I decree that I am my perfect sound of creation. This sound directs my every thought and all my feelings.

> Through the Divine Higher Presence of God, I decree that the Grail mysteries are now raised in my waking consciousness and I now reveal these Codes to the world.[8]

By consciously connecting to Venus and asking that this beautiful planet's energy be integrated with each member's consciousness, personalities would automatically begin to soften, allowing the Codes to come closer to the surface for discovery.

Most of the group effort in ritual and ceremony had to be focused on tending to the moment and making sure that each member's disposition was truly of the highest. Kindness and love projected toward one another had to be "the medicine of the moment".

Excalibur was to be given to each to hold during this Journey. We were to stay pure, calm, centred, and in the Light of higher truths at all times, and Excalibur's power would guide the group through the obstacles that were awaiting us.

We were to hold a legion of eight angels around us on a daily basis to protect the precious information stored within each breast and a legion of eight Archangels was to be included around the entire group at each of the seven sacred sites.

And so we set off to start our work, confident that we were guided, confident that we were protected.

[8]*Trinity of the Flame Send Golden Light from the Temple of the Grail.*
Transmission received by Dr. Norma Milanovich, Albuquerque, NM, 1997.
Copyright at Athena Leadership Center.

THE ADAM KADMON
- Message from Master Kuthumi -

The term Adam Kadmon is first found in a 13th century Cabbalistic Treatise. He is described as the "primordial supreme man".

In November 1995 Norma held a lecture in London, during which she passed on to us how Master Kuthumi defines the Adam Kadmon:

Many on Earth shall soon be reborn into the heart of the Christos. This shall commence when the Moon is in its glory and the Heavens are aligned with the great time of the awakening. Men and women alike, destined to grace the land, shall adorn a new garment of the Order of the Divinity. Music shall radiate from their auras as they sing the highest tribute to spiritual Law.

These sons and daughters of Light are among the masses now and soon to awaken to their personal transformations.

They shall be the forerunners of the new species destined to walk the land, who shall hear, see and speak no evil. These souls will be seen by all as the bringers of the new horizon for Mother Earth.

They shall command the energies to enfold, within, the union of the male and female counterparts that shall be joined.

They shall be entrusted with the secrets of the Holy Grail and will understand how to birth this knowledge for the world before this decade is complete.

They shall be God-realized first so that their consciousness might go forward and change the consciousness of the world.

This new species shall replicate the form of Master that walked the sacred grounds of Atlantis.

This membership will understand how to manipulate the Light so that all will be healed.

Each will understand the significance of the balance of power and how this action is critical for the world's transformation.

These souls will have been altered through the etheric hands of the Divine and will be sent then through the land like the Apostles of old.

They shall join hands with the masses world-wide for the purpose of transmitting the DNA Coding that lies within them to those who are destined to receive the activation in all corners of the globe.

They shall touch the hearts and souls of the One and know that God's plan is truly being realized.

The souls of the Adam Kadmon are awakening to their destinies now and are soon to embrace the perfection of God's Celestial Plan in its significance for Earth.

These souls are beginning to understand why they are here and will soon have no fear for completing their missions.

Look within and see the Adam Kadmon radiance glowing within your hearts, dear children of Athena, Sananda, Buddha and Quan Yin. Then know that the Path I have described is your Path and the Path of the warriors of old, who came and left their legacies on Earth long before your time. Now it is your turn to take your stand.

I offer you the cup of the Holy Grail, but it cannot be examined for understanding until 1997.

So you are holding this energy now, and you collectively will release it in 1997 for the world so that they can all become self-realized.

Please accept this offering, however, at this time and know that it contains all you need for sustenance until you have been self-realized within the Adam Kadmon consciousness.

God speed you on your Journey, Dear One,

I AM Kuthumi.[9]

[9]Transmission received by Dr. Norma Milanovich, Albuquerque, NM, 1995.
Copyright at Athena Leadership Center.

SITES 1 and 2 - ILE DE LA CITÉ and NOTRE DAME

Photo by Antonio Genco

Our first two ceremonies took us to the Ile de la Cité, the cradle of Paris. This area was first inhabited around 200 BC by the Celtic tribe Parisii whose settlement has become today's Paris.

The Cité of Paris is crossed by two magnetic axes. The first comes from Burgundy and flows in the direction of the Normandy. It crosses the Ile de la Cité. The second connects Reims with Chartres. It also flows through the Ile de la Cité. Where these two streams of energy cross an energy exchange is created. On this point stands Notre Dame Cathedral.

We positioned ourselves in the presence of the Archangels of Power and spoke an invocation that the seven Codes held in our hearts may be delivered to the world.

The following invocations were used at each sacred site.

Gabriel's Trumpet

Joan of Arc has prepared this site.
She has sounded Gabriel's trumpet.
The frequency is now here
to raise our Light vibrations to the note of "A".
The chambers of the Most High are ready.
Receive our collective oversoul.
Standing in the Light of the Great Central Sun hold for us,
Celestial Goddess, the torch that will light this site.
Ignite the Codes that are destined to be released.[10]

Angels and Archangels

Through the portal the Celestial Realms stand ready.
At this sacred site we call for assistance.
Guide our path through the labyrinths of the mind.
A legion of eight Archangels surrounds our group.
Each member holds another eight angels.
Oh, Light Beings of Power, we become one with you.
Unite with us in the ritual we are about to perform.
Guide our path and clear our minds.[11]

For all of our rituals we used various crystals and *holy water* from the Chalice Well in Glastonbury. *Sacred water* from Lourdes was also added towards the end of the Journey.

This *water* was then charged with the energy and Codes of the ceremonies, to be used later during our work in England, America and Australia.

[10&11] These invocations as well as all other decrees, prayers and meditations used during the ceremonies were composed by our spiritual leader, Ron, from the Messages received from Master Kuthumi.

ROUEN

For our Journey the archetype and oversoul of Joan of Arc held the portal open for 14 days while the siege endured. Joan of Arc held the keys for the magic to emerge. She rode ahead of the group to assure that the chambers of the Most High were ready to receive the group's collective oversoul.

We honoured Joan of Arc and made a detour in order to visit the ancient city of Rouen, famous for its medieval wooden-framed houses and a number of churches. In this city Joan of Arc was burned at the stake for heresy. A church was built here in her memory.

We said prayers to Joan of Arc and blessed her with flowers at three sites in Rouen.

Prayers for Joan of Arc

Oh, Joan of Arc.
Three prayers we give thee.
Celestial Goddess, your courage fills us with courage alike.
Your service to the higher realms inspires us to act the same.
The love you give us overflows our hearts.
For these three gifts we thank thee.
For these three we exchange our prayers, of three, for you.
Accept, Celestial Goddess, our gratitude
that once again we may touch the Grail.
Remain with us;
guide us in the days to come.
The work for us continues on.
In our homeland, for each of us,
missions of the Grail await.

SITE 3 - CHARTRES CATHEDRAL

Chartres Cathedral was a great favourite of the group. Its spire, which is called a "cosmic aerial", can be seen from a great distance.

Chartres is a place where the Spirit breathes. In Christian times it was one of the most sought-after places of pilgrimage in France. It is Spirit that one wishes to find on a pilgrimage. Chartres is certainly such a place.

The rose windows at Chartres are a special feature of the Cathedral. The colours and their design radiate great harmony and charm.

On the north porch of Chartres Cathedral there is a statue representing Archangel Melchizedek holding the Grail Cup.

HIDDEN STREAMS OF SPIRITUALITY

You can see it for miles; its spires dominate the skyline. Situated south-west of Paris in the rolling fields of the Eure-Loire valley in the province of Normandy, Chartres Cathedral is the home of the medieval mystery school and more than a temporal edifice. It is a glorious monument to the enduring truths which lead man closer to Source.

© Painton Cowen   Chartres North Window

Arriving in the late afternoon's fading sunlight on December 12, 1997, I was still unprepared for the absolutely superluminous quality of the stained glass windows that grace Chartres' granite walls. The Light that emanates from these medieval works of art cast iridescence in the shadowy confines of the interior cathedral itself. The glass was made by medieval craftmasons, using secret knowledge brought back by the Knights Templar from Jerusalem in the twelfth century. This lost process creates a wavelength of Light, which harmonizes with the natural vibrations of human cellular tissue to maximize the effect of the initiation experience. I, for one, was transfixed, bathing in its glow.

Dr. Malcolm Miller, long-time resident guide and the force behind the mammoth stained glass restoration project, took us through the Cathedral. At one point, our group was seated while Dr. Miller spoke to us of the pictorial history of the glass and the church itself. When he spoke of the Labyrinth, for which Chartres is so famous, I asked where it was and if we might walk it ourselves. He pointed directly at my feet! I was standing in the centre of it and had not known. Fifteen rows of folding chairs had been unceremoniously positioned directly over the Labyrinth, leaving only a narrow isle running through the maze itself. Now, no one could walk it, unless all the chairs were moved. At that point, I mentally walked the Labyrinth. As I did this, I threw a Violet Flame over the area to assist in starting a releasing process so that anyone making the pilgrimage to Chartres could walk the Labyrinth at any time.

As this stop on our itinerary was the third point to activate, the theme of the meditation centred on the principle of Vital Energy, representing the Third Chakra of power and self-esteem. As we stood meditating with white tapers in our hands, I thought how appropriate this was. Outside, the city of Chartres was decorated in holiday splendour, a living testament to the power of Light over darkness. Our four-block walk to the Cathedral itself had given me an otherworldly feeling of having been here before in a procession, holding just such a Light. Had we all been together here in another time, holding the Light, just as we were now doing? I think so.

As daylight faded, we again boarded our bus, to be whisked away to our next stop. However, the Light of Chartres' glass and the initiatory experience of its Labyrinth linger. I believe Chartres holds a key to the Music of the Spheres within its walls. Combined with the underground streams of the Eure river and the illumination of the stained glass, much more awaits re-discovery by humanity. Our task, it is clear, was to activate the portal, in preparation for that time -- soon to come. I feel truly honoured to have been a part of this.

(Lynne)

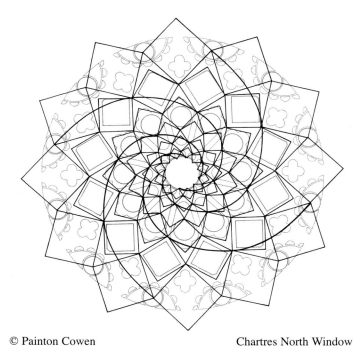

© Painton Cowen   Chartres North Window

HARMONY OF THE SPHERES

Geometries within geometries
Reflecting from the realms of Light
Into the world of form.
Cascading grids through dimensions
Beyond space and time.
Crystalline templates of worlds within worlds
Carrying the sacred languages
Mathematics, sound and colour
Spirit's movement to create
Infinite Life
Infinite Love
Infinite Divinity.

Rose Windows opening
Their eternal circles to the sun
Shining forth their symmetry
In radiant jewelled patterns of unity
So the gateway of each soul's heart
Opens to God's living Light
Unfolding its petals as the rose
Before its glorious face
Bringing the perfection of Divine Love
The Harmony of Joy.

We walk the Labyrinth of Life
The rhythm of One Heart
Three, two, one, four, seven, six, five.
Returning to the centre of our Being
We find the Alpha and Omega
THE ONE

(Felicity, London, September 2000)

29

SITE 4 - MONT ST. MICHEL

This isolated granite cone, almost 80 metres high, rises abruptly from the sands with the ancient Abbey perched on the summit.

Throughout its history the Mont has been closely entwined with spiritual legend and religious orders.

Our ceremony was carried out here in the most beautiful late afternoon Light on the steps to the Abbey.

Afterwards we followed Master Kuthumi's request and displayed as guided our own individual symbols, which we had received before the Journey and on which we had meditated for many weeks.

These had to be laid down from left to right in four rows. We were told that the symbols that the group of 48 Knights of Old had brought through collectively comprised the total library of symbols for humanity's access to the higher Codes of the soul.

After our return home Archangel Metatron gave us a further explanation about these symbols, which had to be combined with truths and numbers.

> The combination of these energies is indeed ancient and strong.
> A long time ago, at the very beginning of time itself when the early beings, who were the founders of mankind, lived upon the planet, they were taught about the powers and processes of creation by the angels themselves. The only way that the angels could explain to them the mystery of this magic, so that their minds could absorb the truth, was by translating these mysteries into symbols and sounds and mathematical truths.[12]

[12]Channelled by Edwin Courtenay, London, 31.1.1998.

In Search of the Holy Grail

Grail Symbols for Accessing the Higher Codes of the Soul.

These symbols were collectively brought through by 48 souls who journeyed to France in December of 1997, under the tutelage of Ascended Masters Kuthumi, El Morya and Isis to recapture the secrets of the Holy Grail. Contained within these symbols, for each person on Earth, are 3 symbols, unique to his or her soul, that once understood, provides the keys for opening up the passageway to the Ninth Dimension, illumination, and the secrets of the Grail Mysteries.

In Search of the Holy Grail

Grail Symbols for Accessing the Higher Codes of the Soul.

In Search of the Holy Grail

Grail Symbols for Accessing the Higher Codes of the Soul.

35 UNITY · LOVE · UNDERSTANDING · HONOUR

BRINGING THROUGH OF THE TRUTHS

Master Kuthumi had warned us that this Journey would not be as easy as the other Journeys in the past. He had hinted at what this might imply by using the words "maze" and "the labyrinth of the mind".

En route, Master Kuthumi instructed us on the truths we needed to bring through and began by saying:

> Each member must continue to hold nine truths that his or her soul understood when making the commitment to hold the mysteries of the Grail. These nine truths are all contained within each symbol that has been held within safe-keeping for the last many centuries....
>
> Following today's ritual at Mont St. Michel the Knights of Old, who begin to unlock the portal to the higher dimensions of time/space, are asked to record only six of the truths that will be remembered. By the Journey's end, each must record the full nine.

After we had displayed our symbols at Mont St. Michel, Master Kuthumi connected with us again:

> I begin by lighting the way to the Great Central Sun by projecting a beam of golden Light from my Third Eye to the Temple of the Grail in the mind of God. I do this to position my electrons in the "Ninth Dimension", which will allow the higher truths to flow.... Completing this step connects the pineal gland of the central nervous system with the mind of Isis and locks a grid pattern around the soul, enabling it to travel on a higher electron spin frequency.
>
> It is the soul that searches for the Grail, Dear Ones, and not the physical self. It is the soul, therefore, that one must consciously enter in order to comprehend the mission at hand....
>
> The process the group is presently following provides an arena for each to measure how pure one is today and how free of judgment each has become. That is why each has been asked to journal their truths. Truths recorded will reveal the volume of Light presently registering in the soul. How pure the truths are will reveal the purity of the Light within the soul also.
>
> Those truths that stand the test of time and emerge victorious after scrutiny and debate become the steps to follow to obtain Christ consciousness and the Grail. The final list of truths holds the Keys for exciting the electrons in the pineal glands which will activate the Codes destined to reveal the Grail mysteries. In

34

truth there are only three Grail mysteries that need to be revealed to the world. These three Keys, once understood and recorded, carry the frequency that unlocks the power of co-creation within the soul enabling one to see through the mind of God.

Connect one's Third Eye as defined above. Then, with new programming flowing through one's consciousness, begin to reduce all to the Trinity Concept. The Trinity comprises the existence of all there is -- just begin to think like a God or Goddess and all shall be revealed. Holding one's attention on the connection between the Temple of the Grail and the Third Eye brings forth the ninth dimensional concepts that reveal the keys to life. They are simple, pure, concise and yet profound, for they contain the knowledge stored in the Egyptian Ankh, Moses's staff, and Mother Earth's auric field. Take as long as the group needs to complete this step of the process. Considering this small task has not been adequately completed since the days of Atlantis, adding a few more days in the process does not seem to be an unrealistic addition.

Our spiritual leader, Ron, composed from the Message received from Master Kuthumi the following beautiful Grail Meditation:

The Meditation of the Grail

I detach from all things connected with the five senses.
I hold no judgment and stand detached from the physical world.
I project a beam of Golden Light from the Third Eye to the
Temple of the Grail in the Great Central Sun in the mind of God.
Travel freely, oh my soul, to the higher mind of God.
Touch creation.
There, my soul, search for the Grail.
With my higher mind connected to Isis, I meditate on the Grail.
There, three truths only I will find to be revealed to the world.
I allow the new programming to flow through my consciousness.
I reduce all to the Trinity Concept.
I think like a God or Goddess.
All is revealed to me.

This time Master Kuthumi came through with the assistance of Isis and shed further Light on our Quest:

I begin by completing the Grail Meditation and do so to complete the will of God and activation of my own etheric pineal gland. In the mind of God is the electron that is replicated on the microcosmic level in humanity's collective mind. This electron is reduced further to the Tachyon energy particle of the universe. The Tachyon energy unit is the Light that connects all within the crystalline web of creation called the electromagnetic grid. In order for any human to become one with this cosmic creative force, one must become that Light particle which resonates to the tone of "A" in the pineal gland. Once an individual can maintain constancy in being this tone, he or she becomes the vibration of the Christ, which is universal love and also the frequency of creation. On the Tree of Life this frequency resides above Tiphareth, which represents the heart connection to the creation process and the embodiment of unconditional love....

He advised us:

The more each member now conducts the Grail Meditation, the more the soul will be activated in the Light to resonate fully on the higher dimension. Continue practising this exercise, even after this Journey is complete, and your souls will continue to soar into the informational channels of this higher dimension of time and space.

Master Kuthumi informed us:

There is a pattern of activation for accessing all higher information and truths that is unique to each soul in embodiment.

>*This unique pattern has Codes that represent:*
>>*three symbols unique to each individual,*
>>*three direct truths that represent that individual's divine programming on Earth, and*
>>*three numbers that correlate to the two above,*
>>*after a symbol is set that designates each truth.*

Once this combination of Keys and Codes is discovered for each individual, that soul can use those consciously to travel to the "Ninth Dimension" and retrieve all higher truths and wisdom for his or her path and for service to humanity.

>*The Trinity that each group and individual must design is the Key to the Grail....*

>*The symbols that the group of 48 Knights of Old collectively have brought through comprise the total library of symbols for humanity's access to the higher Codes of the soul. There is one Code missing -- by design....*

36

The three symbols each member needs to reclaim his or her unique formula are all contained within the full spectrum of 48 that will be brought forth.

Therefore, the symbol presented by each member represents one third of his or her own soul's programming.

The other two symbols are already represented, or one still could be the missing symbol.

I, Kuthumi, reveal today that Isis holds the Key that will reveal the final symbol.

Not all who wish to know these Keys and Codes will be granted access to discovering all. That is so because all souls must be tested to assure they can handle the power and responsibility that comes from having access to the "Ninth Dimension". Only the highest adepts are granted this cleared passageway, for only those souls are cleared to work with the mighty Elohim -- the true creators of the universes. Therefore, only those souls who have been strictly tested will be granted the knowledge of the Divine's Plan....

One's perfect sound is the stillness and sound of creation, which must be activated through one's connection to Isis, Venus, and the perfect breath within. For the souls who continue to practise achieving this connection in the months to come, they will find that they will quickly begin to bring through higher truths at an astounding rate. For those who succeed, the five-pointed star, whose point faces the heavens, will become integrated permanently into their Third Eyes and they will be sealed with the Star of Abraham, preparing to serve the world and working to unite the Twelve Tribes of Israel in the years to come.

The Grail is wisdom contained within the divine Light of God, Dear Commanders of Old. It is the Light of God that provides each the passageway to retrieve all higher sacred knowledge and to bring this forth, in service, to the world. Only humanity can co-create with the mind of God and only humanity can co-create with the mighty Elohim to bring the Seventh Golden Age on Earth.

Camelot *and the universal Cities of Light are one. The Cities of Light are comprised of people who hold this Light. Wherever this Light co-creates the Divine Plan on Earth, a City of Light,* ***Camelot,*** *is born.*

The 48 Knights who have assembled in this sacred valley of the Languedoc represent the Order of Melchizedek High who carry the first true Keys of co-creation within their hearts for creating the Seventh Golden Age on Earth. Each member represents the spark of Light of the mighty Elohim and each will find in the future that his or her responsibilities will continue to grow. Begin today to form a clearer vision of your paths and destinations by projecting first a 12 month and then a 24 month plan emanating from the Heart Centres. Then, visualize each day the ideal situation for tomorrow and walk into that dream. In the dream is all wisdom on how to create it. In the wisdom is the creative energy of thought and manifestation. Hold onto the dream and become regular visitors to the "Ninth Dimension" and Ye shall permanently become residents of Shamballa....

Move not your electrons from the Temple of the Grail....

Continue expressing love in any way your soul needs to do so, and victory is assured.

Adonai in the Light of the Most High.

I AM Kuthumi.[13]

[13]*France Journey, First, Third and Fourth Message Received Enroute.*
Transmission received by Dr. Norma Milanovich, Albuquerque, NM, 1997.
Copyright at Athena Leadership Center.

HOLY GRAIL

I AM a Cup of Light
Radiant I AM
In the love of Divine Being
The Truth of perfect expression
Eternal Light shines forth.

I AM an open Vessel
Abundant I AM
That the purity of Life
May fully flow
In its mighty Cosmic Power.

I AM a sacred Geometry
Perfect I AM
That Spirit may move with grace
In its holy directions
To create forms of Love.

I AM a pure Heart
Love I AM
The door wide open in devotion
In gratitude and praise
To the God of my Being.

I AM the Holy Grail
Sacred I AM
Love's Divine expression
Spiralled into form
Holy and whole I AM the WORD.

I AM THAT I AM
EHYER ASHER EHYER
AIN SOPH

(Felicity, London, November 1999)

SITE 5 - CARNAC

At Carnac the ancient megalithic stones greeted us in brilliant sunshine. The colourful landscape appeared more like early Autumn than deepest Winter.

Visitors to the megalithic stone-fields during the time of the Summer Solstice have reported profound experiences, like unusual clarity of mind, creative abilities which had not been apparent before, a deep love originating from the innermost core, an intense connection with nature, a spiritual awakening, an unexpected gaining of energy and dynamic, or a physical, psychic and spiritual cleansing.

Here, through video-filming, we were given evidence that we not only travelled under the guidance and the protection of the Spiritual Hierarchy and the Archangels, but that we also were accompanied by a number of spaceships, which were not visible to the human eye, but were captured by the lens of the camera.

The memory of our ceremony at Carnac is a particularly moving and precious one.

THE STONES OF CARNAC
WITNESS THE HEALING OF LOVE

The morning that we were scheduled to visit the powerful rocks at Carnac was intoxicated with intrigue, promising the remembrance of something long forgotten. And when we arrived at the first site, the air was filled with an essence of mystery such as that which the sword, Excalibur, always held.

All the participants of this sacred Journey were called "Knights" by the Masters who were guiding our Journey and we soon adopted the template they had woven around us, calling one another Knights like we were all old comrades reunited. "All for One and One for All" became the new chant and theme for our merry group. And when we would joyously sing our slogan aloud, we would commandingly lift an invisible sword up in victory.

One of the Knights had actually brought a full-sized replicated sword with the name "Excalibur" engraved on it. It was truly magnificent and it made me laugh -- it had such a power about it.

That morning a few of us decided that we should carry the sword around with us to empower our Journey and meditations that day.

We looked at the rocks from a distance because there was a fence separating us. They were like incredible beings, each one. Some of them were huge, three to four metres high and almost as wide. They had faces and a powerful energy about them. They were individuals with a unique personality all of their own.

We filed through the little organized museum displaying beautiful photos. For centuries people had speculated on how the stones were placed there and if they had any special purpose. No one really seemed to know the mystery of their enchanting presence in this quiet countryside. We were filled with awe, but were forced to remain separated as if from old friends. Not to be able to touch these magnificent beings before us seemed a torture, and we sadly lamented.

It was my turn to take the sword next and hold it close to me while we drifted around the site. I was happy to have it against my body under my heavy parka, and I was sure I could feel the power of Excalibur and what it meant. I walked into the nearby forest and felt the force of the huge trees. I saw how the elemental kingdom, the plants and minerals, held a tremendous magical healing power that we could tap into whenever we wanted or needed. It was at our command -- there always, for our use. And in that kingdom seemed to be the great secrets of who we were. I wandered back to the fence which kept us away from the great rocks. I pressed my face up against the wire and I wished I could hug them all, even as I felt the sword, Excalibur, at my heart.

Then, to our surprise and relief, we discovered that there was indeed a nearby site where there was no barrier to prevent us from walking amongst the great rocks. A local resident had obviously heard our prayer and had mysteriously appeared to guide us to this place. We rushed to board our bus in anticipation of having a real experience with these amazing rocks found throughout the area of Carnac. As I stepped on the bus, I handed the sword to the Knight who had become an integral part of my Journey in France. It was his turn to carry Excalibur.

Why we were led to do this, I had no idea. We were just following our intuition, which had seemed much easier to do since we had begun our Journey together in Paris. Living in the moment had become common and comfortable for us all. We were magically lifted into a place where it seemed natural for us to listen to our inner guidance, trusting our intuition explicitly no matter how illogical or strange it might seem to our mind. It was all part of being in the "Ninth Dimension". It was a place we operated from, where we were totally connected to God, Source, Spirit, our Higher Power, whatever you choose to call it. And it was an amazing, joyous and fulfilling place to reside in. It was a gift that was given to each of us who were called to be a part of this sacred Journey. And in the end, it was truly a Journey to our Selves.

Soon we arrived at our chosen place, and what a site! The rocks were awesome. And we could actually walk around them, touch them, hug them, love them. The atmosphere was charged with a vibration like no other. I looked around and knew there was a Presence so high and so beyond what we could understand that I did not even try to comprehend it. I knew some intelligence that I could not grasp was with us, somehow sharing this profound experience through us. I even said to myself, "I know you are there." Who "they" were that I referred to, I wasn't sure. Was it the guidance of Angels, Ascended Masters, Saints or divine Spirits? Or was it the presence of great beings from other worlds?

The exchanges with the huge stones were beyond powerful. They held an essence, a wisdom, a message. Each of us experienced a connection with these ancient beings that was meant to be. It felt as if the rocks were waiting for us to reunite with them once more and to receive their vibrations of knowledge -- the truth of who we are. That's what they gave us -- fragments of ourselves.

When I hugged them, there was an exchange of our energies and then we merged. There was no separation. We were one. The stones activated something so deep within us that it is hard to explain in third-dimensional words. If this recollection is blessed enough to carry a thousandth of the impact and frequencies those stones imparted, then you may feel the power.

We gathered around to do our meditation and it was fitting that our circle ended up being heart-shaped because of the position of the trees and stones. We had been led to an unmarked, unfenced place in which we were the only visitors. We had the whole place to ourselves and we somehow felt Home.

The theme of our prayer was Oneness and the connection we all share on this planet. We meditated together, the Great Stones and us. I saw the two Knights across from me for whom, together with myself, a very strong past life memory had been re-awakened on this Journey, which rang with old, ancient feelings of love and betrayal. Sound familiar? The triangle of **Camelot** -- Arthur, Guinevere and Lancelot.... I felt pain in my heart once more and then I felt a great need to forgive him, to forgive her, to forgive mankind, and to forgive myself.

After the meditation we dispersed, going our own separate ways to interact with the stones and to have personal experiences again. Suddenly, I found myself next to my two fellow Knights -- the man and woman. He still held the sword which I had carried earlier. Of all the places to be, why had we ended up together face to face in the same place in this vast field of stones?

The man then planted the sword, Excalibur, in the hard, cold Winter ground. I saw the great blade and the intricately engraved handle. I stood erect and suddenly felt Excalibur as my own body. The guard of the sword was horizontally across my shoulders, the handle going up the back of my neck and head, and the blade running down my spinal column, aligned with my Chakras. I *was* Excalibur, the Power of God. *I knew the truth.*

I had a strong feeling that the man had the same vision. I silently held the hope of love and forgiveness. Then the three of us embraced. In that precious, glorious moment we three stood together in complete love. It was one of the most powerful moments of my life, because I felt forgiveness and unconditional love within myself, between us and with all mankind.

We healed the triangle of **Camelot** there amidst those witnesses, the awesome stones of Carnac. The Cities of Light, **Camelot** can be fully realized once more, here and now, not just because of this one instance, but because of many who are all working for the same vision -- Brotherhood, *Oneness and the Love, Wisdom and Power* within each of us, the truths of the Holy Grail.

"All for One and One for All".

(Kate)

THE ORIGIN OF THE KNIGHTS TEMPLAR
AND THEIR MISSION
- Message from Master Kuthumi -

By now the first half of our Journey lay behind us and we were on our way to the Cathar and Templar Country.

The following text describes the origin of the Knights Templar and their mission:

> Joseph of Arimathea was a member of an Order known as the Violet Robe. The Order of the Violet Robe had existed since the time of Lemuria. These were priests who were given instructions directly from the Divine or the angels themselves in order to guide mankind towards the fulfilment of their potential and their truth.
>
> The Order of the Violet Robe in later parts of history became known by many different names, one of which was the Knights Templar, one of which was the Cathars.
>
> The Order of the Violet Robe in all its shapes and forms has been dedicated to guiding mankind towards the unfoldment of its enlightened potentials and capabilities.
>
> From time to time the power of the Holy Grail was still needed, and those who were affiliated with the Order of the Violet Robe would journey to Glastonbury and to Joseph in order to take from the Holy Grail some of the water and the blood that never seemed to need replenishing, that remained eternally in the cup, and sometimes, too, the chalice itself was borrowed, was taken by other members of the Order of the Violet Robe to other parts of the world in order that its force, its power, its magic could be used.
>
> One of the places that indeed it was taken to was France. Its energy was utilized there to sustain and erect a powerful underlying energy-field that was impregnated, that was planted into the land itself.
>
> When the Grail was taken to France in order that it should be used in this way, it was assigned protectors, people who would keep it safe and people who would, when the time was right, participate in a ritual that was required to tap into the Grail's force and power in order that the Etheric Temple may be created. These people had to be pure of heart in order to access the Grail's fire, the Grail's holy power.
>
> These Knights were members of the Order of the Violet Robe, were connected to that group that at a later date would be called the Knights Templar.[14]

[14]Channelled by Edwin Courtenay, London, 3.9.1997.
See discourse *The Spiritual History of the Holy Grail* p.6.

SITE 6 - RENNES-LE-CHATEAU

After a long bus drive south we entered the valley of the Languedoc. Much has been written over the years about the mystery of Rennes-le-Chateau and its surrounding countryside.

Master Kuthumi had provided us with the following information about the area:

> In ancient days, when the Grail was taken to France, an energetic Temple was established here in order to preserve and protect a powerful underlying primal archetypal force and energy that was under threat from the negative bombardment of thoughts and emotions that were being poured into it by those people that resided upon it now. As is always the case, Light attracts darkness and this place of original Light had attracted a great deal of darkness indeed.
>
> This place was one of the remaining original pieces of land that a long time ago had constituted Lemuria. It was a place that contained the vital force of creation. It was a land that was impregnated with the power of God's love.
>
> This force -- it was known -- would be needed for the future, if the Earth was to enter into its final stage of evolution and enlightenment, and so the Grail's protective powerful energy was utilized to erect an Etheric Temple that would sustain and protect this power, that would enable, in time, the Christ consciousness and the Christ energy to return to the Earth.

You are returning to this place now because we are approaching the time when the energy stored within this geographical location will be raised and actualized, in order that it may be utilized to bring about the rebirth of our society, of our reality of this globe. The energy needs to be prepared. The creation of the Etheric Temple allowed the force, the creative cosmic divine love energy, to be stored, locked in another dimensional locality, existing in the same space and at the same time as everything else, but slightly in a different vibrational dimensional location.

It is time now for that energy to be primed, to be pulled closer. But in order for that to be done, the land itself needs to be cleansed and prepared in order to make sure that there is no negative force or energy that could impair or damage the creative force of the Divine that exists there. This initial Journey, then, is to partially awaken your subconscious and energy body consciousness of your previous incarnation and the knowledge that it possesses of how to utilize the energy of that geographical location and the energy of the Grail itself, and to prepare the land for the return of the energy that will come soon, to cleanse and clear the space in preparation for what will come, to begin to call back the love energy of the Divine, and to utilize once again the power of the Holy Grail to initiate this miracle and wonder.

You are embarking upon your Journey in order to assist the Divine in this, our cosmic task. It is asked of you to assist the Masters, the angels and God in this way, to utilize this understanding in complete compatibility with the understandings that you will be given throughout your Journey and your Quest to perform God's will.[15]

Of great interest are the findings of David Wood, who reveals in his book *Genisis*[16] that there is a Temple imprinted on the landscape of this area.

The result of his work over many years was the recognition and identification of an immense geometrical figure, the figure of the Pentagram, indelibly marked on the ground. He states that this geometrical figure covers an area of over 40 square miles and that every point is marked by a mountain top, a church, or an outstanding rock feature.

Here we have the perfect example of

"As above, so below".

[15]Channelled by Edwin Courtenay, London, 3.9.1997.
[16]*Genisis – The First Book of Revelations* by David Wood. The Baton Press, Tunbridge Wells, Kent, 1985.

THE CIRCLE OF CHURCHES : PENTAGRAM : MERIDIAN

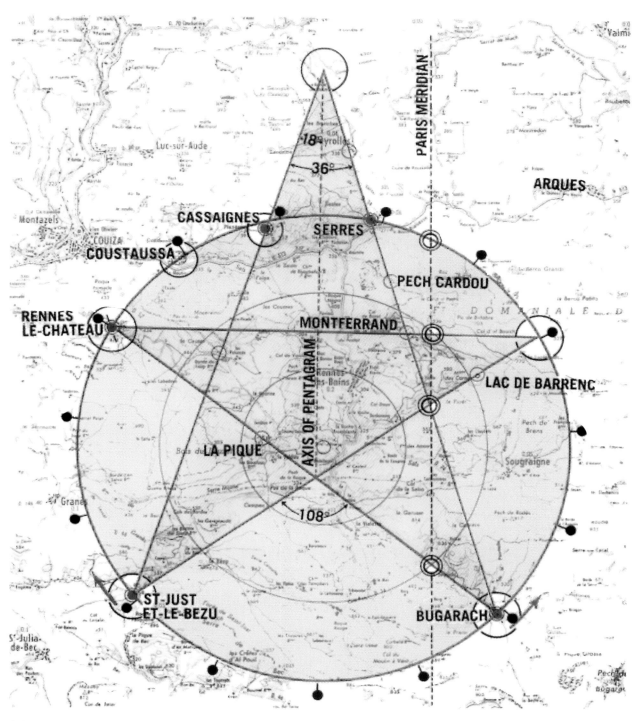

After visiting the church and the Villa Bethania, the group gathered in the garden at noon for the sixth sacred site ceremony.

We honoured the balancing of the masculine and the feminine energies by adding this poem to our ceremonial invocations.

CREATION

Divine Love -- he calls from the sun.
Divine Will -- she calls to his heart.
They blend at the dawn to bring forth their creation.
He gives her his love. She shares her power.
And they call the child wisdom.

(Jill, Margaret River, December 1997)

SITE 7 - MONTSÉGUR

The highlight of our Journey in France was, without a doubt, our visit to the ruins of the castle at Montségur.

Montségur Castle, surrounded by the most majestic mountain scenery, was built in 1204 and served as a Cathar stronghold for 40 years. The Castle, built on esoteric lines, is described as a "sacred portal", a bridge that connected Heaven and Earth. Today the ruins of Montségur are as mysterious and impressive as ever.

Our instructions from Master Kuthumi were as follows:

> Co-ordinate the group membership to be on the top of Montségur by dawn on the morning of December 21. Not all need make the climb to the top. If Isis's heart touches the Third

Eye of only 21 at the summit, the Journey will be a success, for these Knights of Old can carry the Codes of the higher plan (regarding what is to be done with the knowledge released) to the others in attendance. Electrons will fly through the Heavens and hold a frequency around the Crown Chakras of all the membership following this expedition. Meditate for a period of 12 minutes here and hold the image of the Grail in the Third Eyes of all those who make it to the top.

Let go of all limitations and fears at this point. Surround the group membership with the energy of pink and gold. Then form 3 circles of Light and focus the image of the Grail 21 feet above the group's centre. Always sing the perfect sound within and know that in holding this for the world that you also assist Joan of Arc to keep the portal open for the Journey.[17]

These texts and others were read to open our ceremony in the meadow at the base of the mountain.

The Portal

The archetype and oversoul of Joan of Arc holds open
for only 14 days the portal for this Journey.
While the siege endures, align with the spirit of Oneness and love.
Ye shall be delivered from harm's way.

The One Focus

In the land of antiquities and dreams,
one focus only shall be this Journey.
Capture the Holy Grail;
return it to **Camelot**.
Let the dream be realized on Earth;
let the Cities of Light be created.
May the Light of the Most High liberate us
as we complete our duty
with honour and glory.

During the darkness of night, armed with torches, 34 Knights then started the stiff climb up this dome-shaped hill to reach the ruins of the castle before sunrise.

---

[17]*Trinity of the Flame Send Golden Light from the Temple of the Grail.*
Transmission received by Dr. Norma Milanovich, Albuquerque, NM, 1997.
Copyright at Athena Leadership Center.

Here, during a 12-minute silent meditation, we held this visualization.

<u>Sunrise on Montségur</u>

Isis's heart touches the Third Eye of each Knight
atop Montségur at dawn this Solstice morning.
Knights of Old,
carry the Codes of the higher plan.
Electrons fly through the Heavens.
Around the Crown Chakras of all on this expedition,
a frequency is held.
All those present now in meditation
hold the image of the Grail in our Third Eyes.
Let go of all limitations;
let go of all fears.
We surround ourselves
with the energy of pink and gold.
In three circles of Light
we focus the image of the Grail
21 feet above our centre.

The remaining Knights below joined us in a synchronized meditation.

At the end of our ceremony we were rewarded by a spectacular sunrise, which set the sky ablaze.

Our mission completed, we descended, our hearts filled with gratitude towards the angelic host for their protection and the Spiritual Hierarchy for their guidance during a most adventurous Journey.

51

Much gratitude was also given to our spiritual leader, Ron, who took us through all ceremonies with much love and wisdom, and who, through the introduction of very special pieces of musical composition, contributed in lifting us to the ninth-dimensional frequency and assisted us in maintaining the note of "A".

And so we drove homewards, holding in our hearts much love and warm appreciation towards Norma, who led us with great expertise through the labyrinth to the Grail and who enabled us to serve on this most Holy Mission.

REFLECTIONS ON THE JOURNEY
– Message from Master Kuthumi –

Master Kuthumi once again came on the wings of the White Dove to deliver his Message regarding the Search for the Holy Grail. He emphasized the significance of the power of the dove and stated that it now guided each of the 48 Knights into their year of great adventures.

He informed us that the Journey was a success, for each of the 48 souls who made the Journey did, at one time or another, reach the vibrational frequency of the "Ninth Dimension".

Then he delivered this guidance for the months that lay ahead of us:

> In the months to come, Venus will begin to play a significant role in the development of consciousness on the planet. Each of the 48 Knights will be likened to the connecting rays of Venus's influence and will be positioned to integrate this energy into many different places on the planet. Many will journey to far-away lands to set the frequencies for world consciousness to change at an accelerated rate. Others will work on the etheric, more in stillness, but do the same for the world's plan. All in all, 1998 is reserved for many truths to be revealed that will come from the releasing of the Codes contained within this membership....
>
> Isis reveals the forty-eighth symbol for accessing the higher Codes of the soul needed to enter the "Ninth Dimension". That symbol is the number "9", the number of completion, and the goddess. This symbol depicts the summation of the 144,000 Spiritual Warriors who will now emerge on the planet, in this glorious year of 1998, to fulfil prophecy. What will be witnessed because of the group mind created by this segment of Lightworkers will be awesome, when analyzed in the annals of history. The great awakening shall begin April 1 of this calendar year, and this membership will become the living Grail mysteries, become manifest on Earth....
>
> All information destined to flow into the 48 Grail vessels who journeyed to France will be shared with a larger population between April 1, 1998 and the Summer Solstice of 1999. This will be the time of major movements on the planet, greater linkages, free-flowing ideas, and laughter and joy not experienced before. It will be the time of reunion and integration, and many will cry when happiness and Light befall their paths.

Isis's essence has merged with the 48 souls who fulfilled their contracts to hold the secrets of the Grail until the time was right for this information to be revealed to the world....

The Grail mysteries will begin to flow into mass consciousness and illumine the minds and hearts of the many who wish to journey to the hallowed halls of Shamballa. The Earth's breath shall be stilled, allowing the higher information to flow freely into the hearts of those ready to receive....

Ride back now into **Camelot** *and return to where your hearts know the truths. Live these truths and Ye shall live the Grail mysteries. Hold the chalice up in celebration and salute the mighty Elohim for their vision, and in so doing Ye shall be celebrating your own Higher Selves.*[18]

[18]*France Journey, Final Message.*
Transmission received by Dr. Norma Milanovich, Albuquerque, NM, 1997.
Copyright at Athena Leadership Center.

© 1985-2002 AD Nanette Crist Johnson

Master Kuthumi

OUR PERSONAL QUEST FOR THE HOLY GRAIL

Master Kuthumi's final words of wisdom to us were the following:

> The key to self-realization will come from one's ability to become still and listen to the sound of stillness within. This step toward illumination takes you back into time when each of you knew how to access this frequency in a fraction of a second. By doing so, in the waking moments of the day, and by connecting to the Temple of the Grail in the mind of God, your souls will find the freedom needed to merge with the energies of Venus and the oversoul of Isis, who has returned to Earth to usher in the Seventh Golden Age.

Master Kuthumi ended his Message with these touching words about himself:

> I AM Kuthumi, known as Parsifal who saw the elusive Grail and who held onto the dream until the dream became realized. It is through your souls, Dear Ones, that my soul is now set free.[19]

He is handing over the guardianship of the Grail to us. Not only does our mission continue in carrying the Coding of the Grail, but also our personal Quest for wholeness, for unity, for Oneness goes on, and what better way to pursue our task than to follow the example and advice of this beautiful Being of Light, who has guided us with such love and care.

Omraam Mikhael Aivanhov, in his discourse on the Holy Grail, describes the Journey towards Oneness as follows:

> Parsifal, setting out on his Quest for the Holy Grail, is the eternal symbol of the adept setting out on the path of initiation. Like Parsifal, who had to make his way through dark forests, battle with awe-inspiring giants and knights and avoid the many snares laid in his path, an adept is required to brave darkness, combat enemies and overcome temptations. Once he had emerged victorious from all his trials, Parsifal was welcomed with solemnity in a marvellous castle whose walls were covered in gold and precious stones. It was here that he was vouchsafed the vision of the Holy Grail. The vision of the Grail is the supreme reward of him who guards faithfully, in his heart and mind, the ideal of obtaining the priceless gifts of the spirit....

---

[19]*France Journey, Final Message.*
Transmission received by Dr. Norma Milanovich, Albuquerque, NM, 1997.
Copyright at Athena Leadership Center.

Cabbalists, for their part, have expressed this idea in the two interlaced triangles of the Seal of Solomon. The triangle pointing downwards represents the descent of the spirit into matter, whereas the triangle pointing upwards represents the tendency of matter to rise and become one with the spirit. In this symbol, the two meet in mid-course and fuse into one. When the spirit encounters matter capable of holding on to it, it no longer tries to escape. In the meantime, however.... Well, in the meantime, a disciple will experience many ups and downs: when he manages to hold on to the spirit for a few moments, he is raised to a state of ecstasy before slipping back into the prose of everyday life. But he must never be discouraged; he must simply start climbing again and, even if he falls over and over again, never give up....

The chalice of the Holy Grail is the symbol of a human being who has succeeded in capturing and fixing the spirit within him....

The dearest ideal of a disciple is to become the Holy Grail and contain and condense the love of Christ. But to achieve this ideal, he must work on his own matter; he must refine it, render it more subtle and more precious so that it becomes capable of vibrating in harmony with the spirit....[20]

And so we hold on to the perfect dream until our dream becomes reality and we merge infused with *Light* into *Oneness* and live *Love*.

[20]Excerpt from the chapter "The Holy Grail" taken from *The Fruits of the Tree of Life* by Omraam Mikhael Aivanhov.
Distributors Prosveta, The Doves Nest, Duddleswell, Uckfield, East Sussex, TN22 3JJ, 1990.

THE KNIGHTS' MISSION
AFTER THE JOURNEY TO FRANCE

At the end of our Journey in France, we took up Master Kuthumi's earlier instructions as to how the work was to proceed in our individual countries of England, America and Australia.

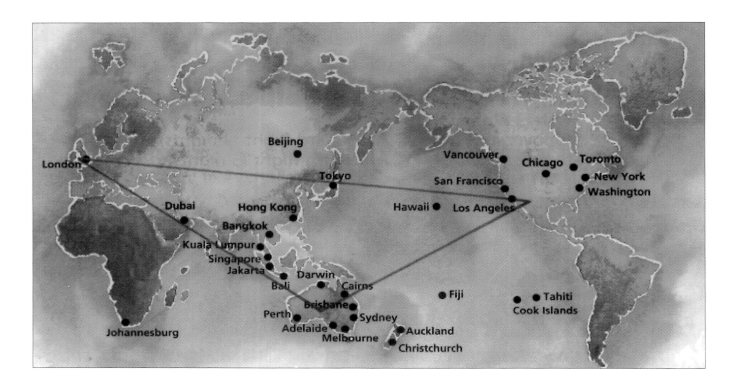

His Message was as follows:

> By the Journey's end and after the Codes of the Grail have been released to the world, gather around the Round Table and formally present Excalibur and the Grail's "gift" of knowledge to the representatives from England to carry back with them to deposit in their sacred land. This latter gift must hold the Keys to unravelling the secrets that the nine Templar Knights of Jerusalem held for the cosmic forces (for these nine Knights will be among the participants on this Journey), the power to set Ezekiel's wheels in motion, and the frequency for the new creations to come forth on Earth.

These Keys and Codes will remain in England for seven months, and be sealed with the Atlantean power symbol -- the Sign of the Seventh Seal. The Knights from England will understand what to do with this gift, even though, at first, their souls may not remember.

Following the completion of the seven-month seal, the England participants must mail the Codes to America and transfer those Keys and Codes through the crystalline electro-magnetic Light grid on Earth, to assure the balance of energy on the planet.

Following another seven-month period, the Codes must be sent to Australia, and the same ritual must be completed.[21]

[21]*Trinity of the Flame Send Golden Light from the Temple of the Grail.*
Transmission received by Dr. Norma Milanovich, Albuquerque, NM, 1997.
Copyright at Athena Leadership Center.

Stonehenge

TEMPLE OF

Not only are the 48 Knights who participated in the Journey linked through their karmic connections, but also the landmasses on which they reside are connected through sacred places of power and the ley-line system.

Stonehenge, Sedona and Kata Tjuta are joined energetically through the Earth and through the ethers. They are points where major vortices are present that serve as dimensional doorways into realms of great Light and power.

The Spiritual Hierarchy emphasizes for us to recognize and understand:

> that as Stonehenge carries beneath it a Star of David configuration, which is connected to the external ley-line energy, these other sacred sites too contain beneath them stars of energy and alignment that connect them to the neighbouring ley-line activity that is interlinked to the vortex in this area.

60

© Bradshaw Colour Studios   Sedona

LIGHT AND POWER

Indeed, Sedona contains beneath it a 7-pointed star and Kata Tjuta an 8-pointed star. Therefore, each is also connected because of the ascending nature of the numerical power of the geometric force that lies beneath these sacred sites.

Aligned together as they are, then, they form three portals, in the centre of which a greater portal is created. Within the space that lies between these three points of Light and power, great energy erupts and is anchored and focused, and although this energy, at this moment in time, is not activated as such, in the future it will become more apparent why this placement is so and what this greater portal of Light achieves.[22]

[22]Channelled by Edwin Courtenay, London, 16.8.1999.

Kata Tjuta

61

PART TWO

ENERGY WORK IN ENGLAND

The 13 Knights from England have taken their missions very seriously, individually travelling to places of power and sacred sites, visiting ancient cathedrals, working on ley-lines, all in order to spread the Keys and Codes we carry.

Some members felt guided to meet in small groups in order to combine their energies and work together.

© Michael Pitts

THE HOLY GRAIL CODES ARE BROUGHT BACK TO
CAMELOT

Our task of bringing through the truths of the Holy Grail completed, holding the vision for creating the Cities of Light, we rode back to England with the Encoded Grail *water,* which was to remain with the English Knights for seven months to anchor the Holy Grail.

Holding Master Kuthumi's focus "to capture the Holy Grail and return it to **Camelot**", it seemed fitting that the first Coding was to be carried out in Cornwall, the ancient home of the Knights Templar and Merlin's Crystal Cave.

Sandy reports on this important day.

Seventh Symbol of the Keys and Codes of Ethics and Morality in the City of Light Camelot

© 1996 Jhadten Jewall - Sacred Spaces

A GATHERING AT ST. NECTAN'S GLEN
(1.2.1998)

Some of the English Knights felt drawn to gather at St. Nectan's Glen in Cornwall, to add our *special water* from France. This area is set deep in the hills and has a cascading waterfall and river. It is recorded as a place where the Knights Templar used to bathe before setting off on a Holy Pilgrimage.

The group gathering consisted of Christine, who had planned the day, Paul, Jane (our tour guide on the France Journey), Sandy and Sally, who composed the *Oneness* tape[23], dedicated to our beloved planet, Mother Earth, and to all those who are assisting in her future well-being.

[23]Distributed by Monsal Tapes, Trafalgar Cottage, Trethillick, Padstow, Cornwall PL28 8HJ, 1997.

On Sunday the sun shone brightly as we set off to reach the valley. As we approached it, suddenly a large hawk (England's closest to the eagle) soared in front of us and up the valley, leading the way. He was instantly recognized as Kuthumi by some of us, and we really enjoyed this extremely unusual and dramatic event.

Upon reaching the waterfall, we put a special crystal into the deep water at its base. We found a place by the river, and we formed a circle containing a selection of crystals brought by each of us, a candle, Paul's small gold and silver sword, the *water* from the France ceremonies, the *water* from Lourdes and some *water* from a special well called Holywell gathered the previous day by Sally and Sandy. This natural spring of Holywell lies deep in a cave in a southern part of Cornwall. We all established that we each felt comfortable with all the items present within the circle.

We became still and Sally sang from the *Oneness* album -- "Wala Cave", "The Dove" and the first and last chants of "The Holy Grail". During the singing Archangel Michael (he channelled this music) appeared holding Excalibur, and from its point five golden rays emanated to the Crown Chakras of the five persons present. We decreed that, if it were in divine order, the *waters* we were about to offer into the river be magnified in their healing power and beneficial qualities 10,000%, and that they be combined as was best into the water of the river and taken where they were meant to go. Then Jane, in meditation, thanked Saint Nectan and the devas and elementals, who were present, for allowing us to use this exquisite sacred space. We placed five drops of each of the *waters* into the rushing river, to be carried forth. Sally conducted a Medicine Wheel that surrounded our circle of crystals, and we each placed crystals from Wala Cave at the various points of the wheel, creating a vortex of Light and harmony and sealing this spot forever. We asked that the spirits of the four directions and those above, below and within bless this special spot we had created.

Following the legend to the full, our obviously (very) bravest Knight, Paul, plunged into the icy mountain water (it was the middle of Winter here) and swam to collect water from the waterfall, accompanied by great cheers from the rest of us. We sincerely hope that he passed an initiation with this great feat of courage!

Sally collects natural quartz crystals from Wala Cave in Cornwall. We used some in the circle and gave some to the river. They had all been linked into one energy of Light. We were also given one each to keep and one for each of the English Knights who were not physically present, to allow them to share in the energy of the day.

We all climbed back through the valley, and, as the sun streamed through the trees, we felt content that a good job truly had been done. Together we had lunch in Tintagel (the home of Merlin's Cave), and a few hours and lots of laughter later, guided by the stars of the evening sky, we journeyed to our earthly homes.

(Sandy)

THE PENTAGRAM
APPEARS OVER ENGLAND

In his last Message to us before the Journey commenced, Master Kuthumi also stated:

> Unlike other excursions into the unknown, the Knights of Old
> who hold the mysteries of the Grail know that their responsibil-
> ities are not complete until the Grail is restored within each
> person's heart. This Journey represents only one step of the
> process and each, upon returning home, must know that unique
> and individual missions await each participant, which will
> require all to carry the Coding of the Grail to other areas of the
> land.[24]

His words inspired me to look at the map of England after our return home, in order to establish where each of the 13 English members lives in relation to the map and which areas automatically would be covered.

Immediately the Pentagram appeared in front of my eyes, and I drew it onto the map and also enclosed it with a circle.

This showed that most members of the group live either on the lines of the Pentagram or within the immediate vicinity, and one member resides on the line of the circle.

(Gisela)

---

[24]*Trinity of the Flame Send Golden Light from the Temple of the Grail.*
Transmission received by Dr. Norma Milanovich, Albuquerque, NM, 1997.
Copyright at Athena Leadership Center.

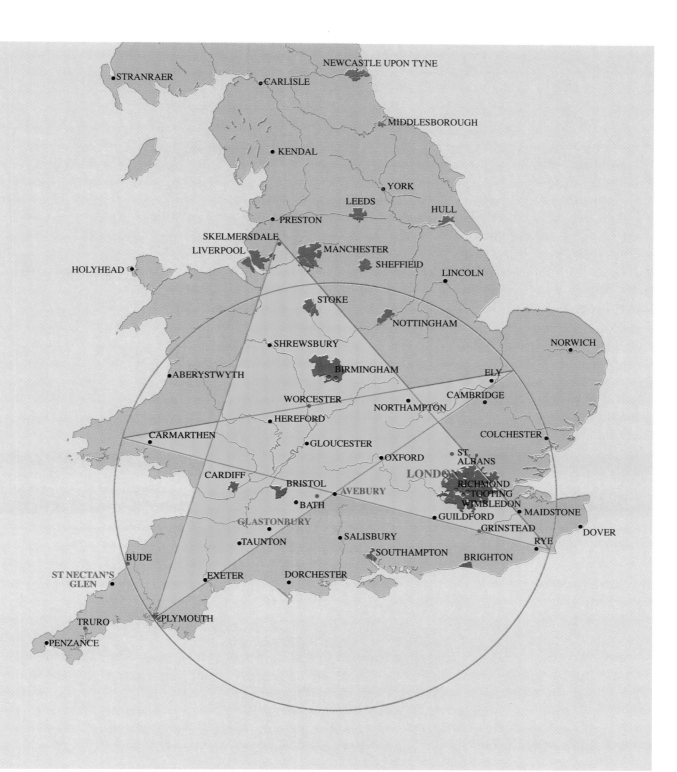

DISCOURSE ON THE PENTAGRAM
- Message from Archangel Metatron -

The symbol of the Pentagram imprinted on the landscape of England, over the areas where the 13 members of our group live, was very intriguing, and the question arose of whether there was any significance in this. At the beginning of February 1998, Edwin Courtenay was consulted again.

This time Archangel Metatron came through and announced himself as "the voice of the Divine, issuer of divine instruction and plan, bridge and mouthpiece for God, representative of the archangelic collective and the angelic collective, overseer of the fulfilment of the divine plan and the enactment."

The following are the words that he offered as an explanation of the Pentagram over England, together with strict instructions for us to follow.

From his Message, it appears that we were involved in carrying out the same task as the royal families of Atlantis over 10,000 years ago.

> We must begin by explaining a little more concerning the powers and the symbols attributed to the Pentagram.
>
> Indeed, as you have been told, the Pentagram is a seal, a capsule, that holds inside it the energetic encodements of the new man. It is, however, more than this, a multi-dimensional symbol, which contains within its structure, its energy, its significance many meanings and many purposes.
>
> The symbol was chosen to hold the encodements for the new man because of its balanced energetic qualities. It is a symbol that represents both masculine and feminine polarity and forms. It is a symbol that represents fertility, inspiration, instigation, as well as nurturing and the capacity for recreation, metamorphosis, rebirth, transition and regrowth. It is a healing symbol that balances the masculine and feminine forces together in perfect harmony, representing the sacred marriage of the masculine and feminine in one, the embodiment of perfection and balanced truth.
>
> The five spokes of the Pentagram represent the five major elements of life. The top spoke represents the power of spirit. As you gaze upon the Pentagram, the spoke that is to your immediate top right is the one which represents the powers of water. Beneath it is the spoke that represents the powers of fire, to its left the spoke that represents the powers of earth, and above this the spoke that represents the powers of air.
>
> These points do not fall by coincidence or chance upon those places on the map where people reside and live. These people represent, embody and anchor at this moment in time for this island these elemental archetypes and qualities. They must

investigate further the significance of the element that they represent, the powers that are attributed to this element, and the archangels that watch over them, and they must align themselves more fully to these forces and see the significance of these forces being anchored here by these people in these locations.

The circle itself represents the unending cycle of incarnation, of rebirth, the cycle of the seasons, the cycle of the year, the spiral of creation, the spiral of time, the magical circle that is the boundary that marks the place between the worlds, that shields negative energies from entering into the sacred Temple, and it marks a space where limitation begins to fall away in view of the creative forces of the magic of the Divine.

Indeed, the anchoring and over-laying of this template upon this island marks an opportunity and a beginning for rebirth and healing here, the rebirth and healing of the consciousness of those who reside here and the rebirth and healing of the physical, geographical location of the British Isles.

From this point, energy will be broadcast outwards through the ley-line system, the meridian system of the Earth, the electromagnetic grid, to the outer-lying areas of Britain and also to the other areas of the world, where in time and in turn these special energies will be carried. Those parts of Britain that fall within the focus of the Pentagram and its circle are, however, those places that are to be fully focused on at this moment in time by these elemental energies, in order to trigger off the catalyst that will aid in the transformation of those other areas not encapsulated by its geometrical form.

More understanding will be given concerning that part of Britain that falls within this pattern at a later date. For the time being, this is all that is needed to be understood.

Work that must be done here also incorporates a united effort to establish this circle and this Pentagram through synchronized meditation and visualization, in order to anchor and bring the energy encoded into those personalities from the etheric universe through the etheric blueprints and through the lines of connection that anchor them to their Higher Selves and the greater beings who choose to use them as their vessels at this time.

This is indeed pioneering spiritual work that has been prophesied and spoken of for thousands upon thousands of years. In time, symbols, energies, forces, rays will be brought down within this form and symbol, once the land and the consciousness have been prepared. This Pentagram is the foundation stone, is the landing pad for future energies, forms and entities to incarnate from and find their way into the Earth.

The Pentagram is to be perceived as a three-dimensional object, not as simply a flat talisman. In time, one of you will be given the model, the imagining of what the three-dimensional Pentagram is to look like. Creating the Pentagram as a form will enable you to visualize it more successfully in the future work that you are to do. In the beginning, visualize it for now as it is drawn on the map, lines of interconnecting Light that will join you together and prepare the way.

In love, in Light, in truth we take our leave.[25]

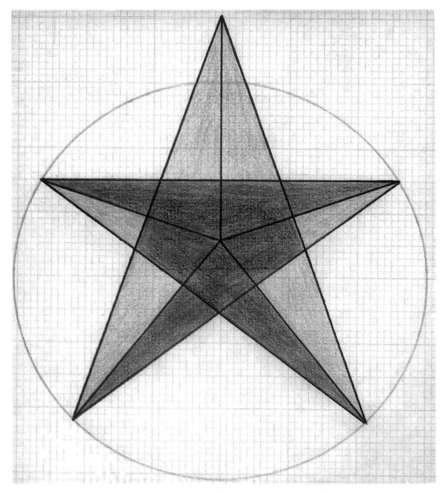

The Pentagram seen as a 3-D object.

[25]Channelled by Edwin Courtenay, London, 31.1.1998.

THE CITY OF LIGHT GLASTONBURY

© 1998 Jhadten Jewall – Sacred Spaces

When it was put to the Spiritual Hierarchy that several of us intended to travel to Glastonbury in order to carry out work there, Archangel Metatron's comment on Glastonbury was this:

> Glastonbury is an area that needs constant work and attention placed upon it. It is still a place of great power and magic, some magic which still sleeps and waits to be awoken, when the time is right. As the Heart Centre of the world, it represents and mirrors the state of the Heart Centres of mankind that exist upon the planet at this time.

At times, it shimmers and shines with brightness that is indeed holy, a compassionate Light, joyous and unconditional. At times it is clogged, polluted, darkened by the darkness of our present society and reality.

It is a beacon that draws to it its polarity opposite and can be equally a place of darkness as it is at times a place of great Light. As mankind shifts and changes, so will the Heart Centre reflect this, and eventually it will once again become the custodian of the holy flame of the Divine.

Energy needs to be projected here to clear and maintain the purity of the Heart Centre, enabling it to vibrate clearly and strongly without hindrance of those who bring to it only confusion and fear and sadness.[26]

Our gathering there became a weekend of great joy. The following is Irene's write-up of the experience.

---

[26]Channelled by Edwin Courtenay, London, 31.1.1998.

THE GLASTONBURY MISSION
(5.4.1998)

© Sarah Boait

The group was told by the Masters that only those Knights of the 13 who felt inspired to journey to Glastonbury to complete work there should go. Their previous incarnational karmic connections obliged and bound them to fulfil this part of the English task. Five Knights felt called: Eileen, Felicity, Gisela, Joan and myself, Irene.

In response to questions asked, the Masters told us that the work that needed to be done in Glastonbury was preparatory. Places of importance and power that had to be visited and cleansed were the Chalice Well Garden, Glastonbury Tor, Weryl Hill, Chalice Hill, Abbey Gardens and the town centre at Glastonbury itself at the memorial site of the central part of Glastonbury town, as well as the sacred oak trees, Gog and Magog.

Invocations and group visualisations calling upon Archangel Michael and Archangel Gabriel were to be made, to provide masculine and feminine forms of transmutation and cleansing. At the Chalice Well and White Spring we were to impregnate both streams with our *sacred water* containing the Keys and Codes.

Our ceremony evolved naturally from the contributions of all the group, and included the five of us forming the Pentagram at each site and consciously representing the elements at each Pentacle, the "Violet Flame Invocation", "The Soul's Commitment", "The Celtic Benediction" (the above three were used during the France Journey), "The Great Invocation" (as updated by Francis of Assisi), Felicity's poem "I Walk", Joan's invocation to the elementals, plus group cleansing visualization and spontaneous sacred additions, which ranged from Aramaic to Sanskrit.

The gang of five were sorely tested by the elements at our first site, Glastonbury Tor. It was as if a physical and psychological challenge were being made to us to dare us to carry out this cleansing mission. The wind blew with all its might, knocking the first in line over (towards the Tor side, I am pleased to report). It took more than this to thwart these intrepid adventurers, who found a sheltered spot at the top, on the easterly side of St. Michael's Chapel. Here the first cleansing ceremony took place. After this successful summit, the wind lost heart and left it to the watery element to accompany us throughout our Journey, assisting us in the cleansing process.

The sacred oak trees, Gog and Magog, were our seventh and last site. With our task accomplished, damp, tired, but exhilarated, we revelled in the mud and danced around our ancient friends. Joan noticed that Magog was growing a fairy tooth and Eileen reminded us how vigorously and sweetly the birds had sung after each cleansing. It was as if they were applauding us for a job well done.

(Irene)

I WALK

I walk in the beauty of the stars
The power of the rocks
The freedom of the wind
The majesty of the mountains
The purity of the rushing streams
The vastness of the oceans
The abundance of the green grass
The hope of the seeds buried deep in the earth
The clarity of the mineral jewels of Light
The directions of the four elements
The unity of all creation.

(Felicity, London, April 1998)

THE CELESTIAL ETHERIC TEMPLE
AND ITS MEANING
- Message from Master Dwal Khul -

Now that the cleansing and clearing at Glastonbury, at the Heart Centre of the world, had been completed, more information concerning that part of Britain that falls within the pattern of the Pentagram was given, the mystery regarding the use of the three-dimensional object that had been created in the meantime was lifted, and we heard more about the nature of the work we were expected to do.

It transpired that, through the visualizations we had been asked to do earlier on the lines of the Pentagram, the Earth was to be primed and readied, and that these visualizations were to assist in the laying of the foundations of a Celestial Etheric Temple. We were informed that this Temple was to be raised and built within the space that is marked on the map of Britain as the Pentagram.

This time, during our visualizations, which were to be accompanied by an invocation, the Pentagram was to be raised from the Earth into the Heavens so that the shape extended from the ground upwards, creating a star-shaped column of energy and Light, with the three-dimensional Pentagram revolving slowly within the heart of the Celestial Temple itself.

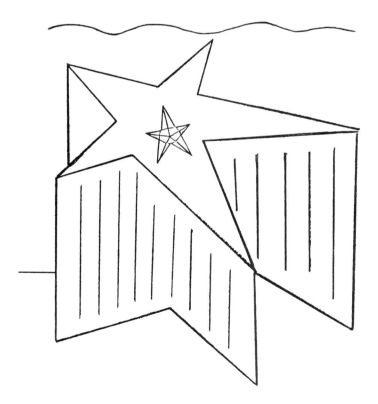

The model of the Celestial Etheric Temple as it was shown to Edwin Courtenay during the channelling of the Message.

In the Message that follows Ascended Master Dwal Khul highlights the importance of the Celestial Etheric Temple:

I am Dwal Khul of the Ascended Masters, Lord of Shamballa, Lord of Order, bringer of peace and sanctity. I am a member of the Brotherhood of Light, I am guardian of the powers of goodness and joy and peace. I come forward surrounded and filled with the blessing and the knowledge and the Light of my brothers and sisters, who shine down upon us from the ascended realms.

I come in accordance with the Divine's wishes and the wishes of the angelic continuum, in order to continue to provide you with the information that you seek at this moment in time concerning further truth behind the powers of the Adam Kadmon Pentagram and also the powers and energies attributed to that particular piece of land that falls within this shape that has been marked towards you within this island of Britain.

The work that we have asked you to do continues through this channelling. There are things now that we would have you do which are of complex nature, things that will, for many, be challenging in accordance with their belief system and their belief concerning their own capacity and power to fulfil the Divine's wishes in this way.

We have enabled you to open yourselves as channels of Light in order that certain Keys of energy could be placed into the Earth via vortex points and ley-line convergence points, so that the Earth would be primed and readied in order to receive the second part of that which we would bring forward at this time:

A creation of a Celestial Etheric Temple that is to be built within the shape of the Pentagram here upon this island on Earth, using the open vessels and channels of those that have been chosen to represent the elemental forces and ingredients needed to combine in order to bring this manifestation into being, in order to make sure that this manifestation occurs and flows in approval with the Divine's consciousness, in approval with the Divine's love and the Divine's will, and of this matter we will talk in more detail in a few moments.

It is important to begin by praising that valiant work that has been done. The dedication that you and your fellow group members have shown is indeed praiseworthy, and noted warmly by the ascended Masters and the angelic continuum and the higher divine cosmic forces that exist.

The energy work that has been done has indeed been most successful in placing valuable Keys, force and power into the vortices and ley-line system of this island, and thereby throughout the Earth, in order to clear and prime certain pathways of energy that they, now raised sufficiently on a vibrational level, may be connected to higher divine templates that exist in the higher strata of the vibrational etheric planes, so that alignments of resonance can occur that will aid in bringing Heaven and Earth into one space and one time.

The energies of the Earth are still low in vibration, but because of your efforts, and the efforts of others that work in other places too at this time, certain key lines of force have been raised sufficiently in vibration to begin to build strands, walls, etheric scaffolding, if you will, that will enable the structure in the beginning of a foundation to occur that will enable an alignment of vibration to manifest in the future.

Without this pioneering and fundamental work, the Earth's transition into a body of Light, into a place of peace and perfection and truth, would not be enabled to occur in the future that is to come. This work, therefore, is vital in the Earth's eventual transformation. Now the consciousness of mankind that will begin to gently rise and bubble, as we move closer towards the point of the Millennium, will begin to aid in the facilitation of the joining of energies that will in time allow the Earth to begin to replenish and heal itself and transform itself into the planet that it needs to become, in order to support the higher Light beings that will transform themselves from their grosser, denser physical selves into their future enlightened beings, as and when the time is right.

This work then is, as was said, fundamental in aiding in the transition of the planet and the transition of the consciousness of mankind that exists upon the planet. It is essential for the future of man.

Within that space marked upon this island as the Pentagram, and utilizing the grace and the open-hearted natures of those people dedicated to the pursuit of spiritual truth and the transition of darkness into Light, a Temple will be raised and built, a Celestial Temple, a Temple that will exist on the etheric plane, a Temple that will be utilized as a gateway, as a doorway, in order that energy may be manifested directly within the outer edges of this space, to fill the space itself with the successful and necessary conscious living thought and emotional energy that will begin to penetrate not only into the consciousness of those people that live within this geometric pattern, but also into the important vortex energies and network of ley-line systems that occur here that will take the energy throughout Britain and throughout the world.

Indeed, other spaces exist on the Earth, vortexes that will be used as catchment areas to receive the energy that will be propelled throughout this planet, throughout the ley-line system, that will aid in the transformation of consciousness, too. But within this geometric outline, within this gateway, within this Celestial Temple, energy will be manifested that cannot be down-loaded into any other place or vibrational climate upon Britain's surface. This energy will not only be in the form of consciousness that will begin to affect and open the minds and the Higher Selves of those people caught within the boundaries of this energy field, but will also be information that will be stored, that will be placed directly into the Light body, into the etheric bodies, into the chakras and into the spiritual connections of the people themselves. The gateway will allow divine templates to begin to be down-loaded through this connection into individuals' consciousness and being. It will allow those who are within the structure to be catalyzed, transformed, quickened, alchemized in order that not only will the energy that emits from this Celestial Temple carry the power to other places and to other people, but that also the people themselves, changed and transformed by the energy, will carry the energy to others who are not so fortunate at this moment in time to live within this space that has been outlined and created.

People will be affected in different ways. Spiritually minded people will advance far quicker than the others. But their consciousness will be gently opened and they will begin to see or act, in their own way, within their own parameters, within their own consciousness levels, spiritual truth that eluded them before.

The creation of such spiritual vortexes, such Celestial Temples has not occurred upon the planet for thousands upon thousands of years on such a grand scale. In the beginning, when the Earth was freshly created, these gateways were utilized in order for certain energy, that was vital for mankind, to reach the desired and necessary evolutionary stages to occur. These Celestial Temples can be seen as energetic white holes, the exit point of spiritual worm-holes, that find their other entrance points in higher dimensional localities. Here energy, information, power, Light and pure spiritual love is poured into the open vortex. This is carried through inter-dimensional states to the exit point that exists now within the Celestial Temple at the physical location upon the planet, allowing the energy to be instantly manifested without being down-graded through the usual channelling processes.

This spiritual dimensional worm-hole, therefore, allows the energy of heaven to enter into the energy of Earth pure and untainted and, therefore, in a much more potent and powerful state. These spiritual worm-holes have always been called Celestial Temples, as Temples were originally places of divine spiritual nurturing and acknowledgement of self-divinity, through the acknowledgement of the Divine as all things external that live and are of Light. The Temple, therefore, provides this opportunity on a more spiritual level through the catalyzation, through the quickening process that occurs.

The Celestial Temple has already had its foundations laid. It will continue to build through the continued efforts of those people who have been chosen to create the Temple on an energetic visualizationary level.

The Pentagram is to be continually, repeatedly visualized, but this time it is to be raised into the heavens so that the shape extends from the ground upwards, creating a star-shaped column of energy and Light. Inside this column, this cut-out shape of energy, of force, of power, the Pentagram is to be seen as you have created it here, a three-dimensional structure revolving slowly within the heart of the Celestial Temple itself, an energetic structure, which will be the core of the gateway, the point from which the energy, information, power, love and Light will radiate and burst forth upon this island and this planet.

Once a week the visualization is to be maintained through a collective visualizing of its structure, form, force and purpose, and indeed I will detail a prayer, an invocation that is to be repeated at this time in order to maintain the substance of the Celestial Temple itself.

From now until May 23 the visualization is to be done, if at all possible, every other day. On May 23 the Temple will be erected, after which once each week the visualization is to be maintained and the invocation repeated. Up until that point the invocation is to be used every time the Temple is visualized by those who have been chosen to fulfil this task here on Earth.

The invocation is as follows:

Raised from Earth to sky, Celestial Temple of Light,
build with love and truth, with faith and trust,
form, take shape.
Build yourself in accordance with the powers
and specifications of the Divine.
Use our minds, our hearts, our bodies
in order that the power may flow,
in order that the Temple may be built.
Open inside a heart, shaped like a star,
an opening, a point of arrival
through which all that needs to be may arrive.
This we ask in accordance with the Divine's will.
Masters and Angels join with us and allow this to be so.

The Temple is the first of many that will occur throughout the planet. They are positioned upon special pieces of land. The land that falls within their pentagramic shape is special, because of its origin or because of the energy origin of that which is stored within its physical structure.

Lemuria, the original land, the part of the Lemurian island that was first created, that gave birth to the remainder of the Lemurian island, was saturated with divine creative force and power. Pieces of this land were taken by the Atlanteans under the Divine's guidance and instructions and deposited in other areas throughout the world. Large chunks of the physical structure of the original Lemurian creative point, which was known as the navel of the world, were removed, using teleportation energies, meta-transference, and they were transferred to other physical locations. All the major continents of the world have a large piece of the original Lemurian energy, the original Lemurian physical structure stored within their centre point.

This is to be utilized now, as we approach the Millennium age, in order to resurrect the transformational energies, the creative energies, that are needed in order to transform the world. The Divine will link to this part of itself still vibrant, still virile, and create a resonant connection, and this resonant connection will enable the Celestial Temples to be built and to bridge the gap between the higher spiritual dimensions and the lower spiritual worlds.

The Adam Kadmon Pentagram, then, represents a number of different things. It represents geometrically, geographically, the divine template for mankind's evolutionary future pattern. It represents the energetic structure of a gateway, a doorway, a Celestial Temple's heart. It represents the encoded energy that will be brought back into mankind and that is needed and necessary in order for us to evolve. It represents our future, it represents our potential, it represents our power.

The creation of this gateway is of vital importance, it is contributory to the transformation of the Earth on a large scale.

We thank you for the work that you have already done and wait in anticipation for the work that you will do. It will be interesting for you, as well as for us, to see the transformations that will occur once the Celestial Temple is built.

In love and Light, in truth,

I AM Dwal Khul.[27]

---

[27]Channelled by Edwin Courtenay, London, 15.4.1998.

THE CITY OF LIGHT LONDON

Our task would not have been complete without carrying out work on The New City of Light London.

Felicity felt inspired to put forward a programme and date for this event.

The following is her write-up of this very special day.

© 1997 Jhadten Jewall - Sacred Spaces

OUR TRUTHS ARE RELEASED AT LONDON
(9.5.1998)

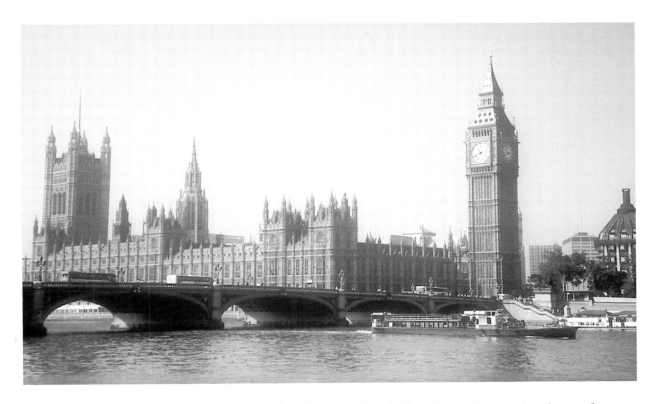

Again, a number of five Knights felt called to gather in London and go to the places of power in the Landscape Temple, joined by the River Thames. It was on a day of special creative energy, two days before the Wesak Full Moon, and the day of Isis's symbol of the nine.

The day came as the first burst of Summer in a blaze of sunshine, warmth and blue sky. It was a joyful, fun-filled day for all of us who were drawn to this task. Joan, Felicity, Gisela, Irene and Steal all duly gathered at 10 a.m., queuing as tourists outside Westminster Abbey. This great Royal Ceremonial Seat marks the Throat Chakra. The crowds were amazing and people could only be let into the Abbey in timed batches. We paid to enter and were shuffled in the human flow around the set route, wondering how we would find the place to do our sacred work, but knowing it would unfold! We were guided to a place in the Cloisters to do our initial preparation for the day, to align and set our intention.

This we did by placing ourselves in the protection of Archangel Michael's blue ray and invoking the Violet Flame.

We then linked with all the group, using Kuthumi's meditations -- three minutes connecting with the hearts of the membership in Oneness in the Golden Light and three minutes projecting the perfected vision of tomorrow in each member's Third Eye.

Then we repeated Kuthumi's three decrees three times each, as we had done in France to hold the note of "A".

Finally we aligned our hearts with Venus, and connected with Isis's seven-pointed star of power, the Adam Kadmon Pentagram (we had been standing in this formation) and the Dove as the symbol of the Trinity of the Grail to show us the way.

"Kodoish, Kodoish, Kodoish Adonai Tsebayoth"*, spoken three times, set the seal on this preparation.

The energies had been beautiful and we were ready to go!

We moved to the centre of the Abbey in the Choir, as near to the nave and transept's cross as we could manage under the watchful eyes of robed guides and with thronging crowds in all directions! Amazingly, we seemed invisibly protected in our energy vortex as we did our first sacred site ceremony of the day.

This format was used at each subsequent place -- there were to be six in all.

We invoked through our I AM Presence a vortex of Light from the heart of Mother Earth to the Great Central Sun, asking the Archangels to protect and surround us as we projected a beam of Golden Light from our Third Eyes to the Temple of the Holy Grail. We recited a Violet Flame Decree three times and then after the "Kodoish..." asked to release the Codes held in our hearts and souls according to the Divine Will as we followed this with a five-minute meditation. The Great Invocation (St. Francis's up-date) was then decreed and the energy sealed in the eightfold seal of Infinity and Light of the threefold Trinity and with the words of the "Kodoish...."

Sounds of many languages were around us and this general mingling with everyone felt an important part of being here. Finally, drinks at the Abbey's coffee bar and sitting down revived us for our next stop, the Thames.

We walked to Westminster Pier and got right down onto a floating marina near Westminster Bridge, where the boats were setting off up and down the Thames and again surrounded by the thronging crowds. We found our place, just after a boat had left, where Steal could put the *water* from the France ceremonies into the Thames without throwing himself in as well! It was not felt appropriate to follow Paul's courageous example! We were in magnificent view of the Houses of Parliament, the Seat of Temporal Power, as we completed our work here and blessed the elementals of the Thames with some loving poetic invocations.

Now the inner child took over and demanded ice-creams and a boat ride down the Thames! Soon we found ourselves on the top of a Thames Cruiser heading up to the City and our next stop, St. Paul's Cathedral. It was a wonderful ride, with perfect views of London's buildings on both sides of us, and as we neared Tower Bridge we saw two large crosses in the sky, formed apparently by aeroplane trails, but very special to us as a sign.

We took a bus to St. Paul's , the head of the Landscape Temple in its surroundings of financial power -- the Stock Exchange, the City Banks. After finding some lunch, we went to do our work in St. Paul's under the dome, where our heads felt the pressure of the intense and powerful energies in our meditation. Then, with help from the angels, we all climbed up 530 steps! These led first to the Whispering Gallery, where we spread out in our five-pointed star formation to whisper our truths. Completing the climb, we went to

*"Holy, Holy, Holy is the Lord of Hosts."

the final heights via iron spiral staircases onto the open balcony that surrounds the Golden Gallery -- the smaller dome above the great one. What an amazing, dizzy-making 360-degree view of the whole City of London! We drank in this panoramic sight on this clear, bright blue day.

It was already late afternoon, and Steal now had to leave us for home and was going to connect with us at 5.15 p.m., when the four women hoped to reach their final site at Kingston, the Heart Centre. Via bus and train we reached Kingston and the Parish Church, where music filled the space -- a rehearsal for a concert, appropriately entitled "Songs of the Soul", with wonderful mellifluous sounds, Heaven-sent. We did our work here timed to perfection to connect with Steal.

Then to the King's Stone, where our hearts felt the energies in the meditation.

Finally, a last determined finish at the Thames bank, again with the *water*.

At 6.30 p.m. the weary Knights fell into buses and trains to find their way back home, tired but peaceful in the feeling of work completed and well-done, and dreaming of hot baths!

(Felicity)

THE GREAT INVOCATION
(as updated by St. Francis of Assisi)

From the point of Light within the Mind of God
Let Light stream forth into the minds of men.
Let Light descend on Earth.

From the point of Light within the Heart of God
Let Love stream forth into the hearts of men.
Christ has returned to Earth.

From the centre where the Will of God is known
Let purpose guide the wills of men --
The purpose which the Masters know and serve.

From the centre which we call the race of men
Let the plan of Love and Light work out
And lift the veil of illusion
Forever sealing the door of darkness.

Let *Light* and *Love* and *Power*
Restore the Plan on Earth.

AVEBURY
- The Keys and Codes Are Transferred Through the Electromagnetic Light Grid -

© Bob Croxford

The seven-month period of duty for the English Knights was drawing to a close. Our individual missions of carrying the Coding of the Grail to other areas of the land completed, we gathered on the eve of our final meeting to reflect on our work and discuss the format of our ceremony.

For this we had chosen the magical place of Avebury. It is here that the lines of the Pentagram over England cross, which shows us that Avebury lies at the womb, the receptive part of this great geometric design.

Preserved by the National Trust, Avebury is a place of undisturbed and ancient creative magical force, a place that sleeps, a place that dreams.

What would have been more appropriate than to gather in the "Fertility Circle" to transfer the Keys and Codes, which we had been holding since Montségur, through the electromagnetic Light grid out into the Earth? From here the energy would be carried smoothly through the ley-line system, throughout the blood vessels and veins of the Earth.

Rejoicing over a job well done, we said our final farewell, knowing that we would all stay connected on a higher level, as we had done for so many lifetimes, until we are brought together again for further work for the planet and humanity.

Good luck to our fellow Knights in America, who were to carry the responsibility for the following seven months, and after that Australia, for the final period.

Our heartfelt gratitude was expressed towards the Archangels for protecting us and to the Spiritual Hierarchy for guiding us and accompanying us through all of our tasks, realizing at the same time that the work carried out not only constituted a service to the planet and to humanity, but also provided every individual involved with an opportunity for personal growth and evolvement.

One week later confirmation was given by the Spiritual Hierarchy through Edwin Courtenay that the Keys and Codes had been placed successfully into the energetic system of the Earth, and that the Etheric Temple had been raised and the blueprint of the great Adam Kadmon down-loaded into the Earth's etheric structure.

FINAL GATHERING OF THE UK KNIGHTS
(New Moon, 23.7.1998)

© Michael Pitts

The Fertility Circle

There were 10 UK Knights present. Jørn from Norway and Torril, an attendee of Norma's workshops, joined us, to add their Light.

We stood, a circle within a circle, with the *sacred water* and the crystal that had been used in the centre circle in France, plus other crystals that were taken on the France Journey.

We began a sequence of meditation steps to ensure that the planet received, in highest order, all that we could give.

Working in harmony, different Knights led different parts of the meditation, in the following sequence:

Invoking Archangel Michael's protection. As we did this, Lord Michael appeared and placed the tip of Excalibur directly into the centre point of the circle, saying "...here is a vortex."

Opening a vortex of Violet Light from Earth to the Great Central Sun -- Violet Flame Decrees, three times.

Linking with the whole group of Knights with Kuthumi's meditations:

1. Connecting with the hearts of the membership in Oneness in Golden Light for three minutes.
2. Projecting the perfected vision of tomorrow in each member's Third Eye for three minutes.

Kuthumi's decrees to hold the group note of "A".

A decree to purify all the Sacred Codes and mathematical programmes we individually carry -- past, present and future, three times.

Opening a vortex of Light from the heart of Mother Earth to the Great Central Sun. Asking the Archangels of Light to protect and surround us as we project a beam of Golden Light from our Third Eyes to the Temple of the Holy Grail in the mind of God.

Silent meditation -- to ensure our connection through our Higher Selves to the very highest levels of universal truth and Light, with each of us individually intending, requesting and allowing that all Keys, Codes and highest truths that were meant for the integration of the Holy Grail into the understanding of humanity -- in highest divine order -- pass down through us and be transmitted to this *sacred water*. We continued our silent meditation, as we passed the *sacred water* to all members of the circle in turn, to allow transferring of Codes.

We then aligned ourselves with the Golden Flame of the Great Central Sun, to pass whatever was required, in highest order, into the planetary magnetic grid system.

"Kodoish, Kodoish, Kodoish Adonai Tsebayoth", three times.

The Great Invocation (as updated by St. Francis of Assisi).

As a final sealing step, we asked that all that was good and holy that each of us had carried from Atlantis, from Egypt, as Knights of the Round Table, and as Templar Knights, and that we had gathered from all four corners of the Earth as we had walked our Journey upon this plane, be taken now into this place on this day, in whatever way was in highest order, and that the energy be magnified ten thousandfold. The event and all the Codes were sealed with the gold Infinity symbol for use in highest divine order.

In our usual style, we raised our invisible swords high to the chorus of "All for One and One for All".

Christine, our UK Codes keeper, then poured some *water* from each of the bottles into the ground at the centre point of our circle.

The rest of that day was spent by most enjoying the wonderful energies of the large number of Crop Circles that surrounded the area.

The BBC1 South TV News on Friday announced an unusual phenomenon. Very occasionally a halo of white Light was seen around the sun. This time the Light refracted and a rare event took place --

"A Rainbow Halo appeared around the Sun".

(Sandy)

EXPERIENCING CROP CIRCLE ENERGIES

In the early hours of July 23, 1998, the day of our final ceremony, this design was discovered at the foot of Silbury Hill, Europe's largest megalithic structure.

© Rod Bearcloud Berry 1998   Silbury Hill, Wiltshire, 23.7.1998

At the completion of our Avebury work Joan and I set off in search of this freshly made Crop Circle.

We walked across a very large field, eager to see our first circle, exhilarated as the outer edges of it appeared. New corn twisted, folded and even plaited into wondrous circles, patterns and designs, surprising us with its detail and intricacy.

We walked to the centre and lay down upon the carpet of corn, smelling its newness and enjoying feeling the energies that emanated from this sacred object. Looking around, we saw others gazing, feeling, measuring and photographing, as if at the birthing of a new-born babe -- the difference being that here there had been no lengthy gestation period; this unique child had been miraculously presented to us fully and perfectly formed.

Reluctantly we left the circle, deciding to climb Silbury Hill before heading for home in order to view it from an aerial vantage point. It was only then that we saw the wonder of the entire creation, complete with four "arms" made up of circles of differing sizes and encircled by numerous smaller circles.

How blessed Joan and I had been to complete the English work and our day in such an amazing way.

(Irene)

THE PENTAGRAM APPEARS AS A CROP CIRCLE

On June 20, 1998, just over four weeks before our final ceremony and shortly after our meditation work on the Etheric Temple had come to a close, this delicate Crop Circle design found a manifestation in the area of Avebury.

Was this given as the earthly counterpart of the Etheric Temple created over England?

© Francine Blake 1998   Avebury/Trusloe, Wiltshire, 20.6.1998

Later, the Spiritual Hierarchy offered this explanation:

> The work that has been done to erect the Etheric Temple has been successful, and the echoing that was seen upon the Earth through the construction of the Crop Circle was indeed a macrocosmic manifestation to indicate that the Temple was anchored and is in place.[28]

This reflection of the unseen world that interpenetrates our own was illustrating

"As above, so below".

[28]Channelled by Edwin Courtenay, London, 29.7.1998.

THE PURPOSE OF THE CROP CIRCLES
- Message from Soltec -

Much wonder surrounds the Crop Circle phenomenon, these meaningful designs, created by the hand of God. The Message from Soltec that follows provides us with some information on their purpose:

Good Morning, Sister. I come as your guide and information expert to provide basic instructions and data that may intrigue you and the minds with whom you may wish to share this information. I AM Soltec, the astrophysicist and ship's communication commander. I speak today for the Tribunal Council of the Galactic Command and welcome this opportunity to come through this frequency to offer another intriguing theory as to the nature of the Crop Circles appearing on your planet.

To begin, the Crop Circles are created throughout the year by the Command to test the soils and the radionic energies that appear on the surface of Earth. The shape of each image left on the surface of the planet creates a radionic surge that penetrates the Earth with such magnitude that it allows us to get a sensor reading on the stability of the planet's electromagnetic nature. These tests are critical at this time, for Earth's electromagnetic flux is unstable. This instability affects not only the planet's ability to hold its present axis position, but also its ability to support life with the crops and food products it provides.

Earth provides foods to its inhabitants by creating paramagnetic vortexes, which attract radionic energies from the cosmic forces. These forces penetrate the soil and terrain. In so doing, the electromagnetic forces combine with the electrolytic fields of Earth to provide "currents of life", as we call them, that support and sustain photosynthesis. In this condition, maximum energy is supplied to plant life and all other energy forms.

Throughout the last few decades, we have observed that Earth is slowly losing its capacity to provide paramagnetic forces that unite cosmic energies with energies on Earth. Therefore, we are creating these designs on the planet's surface for you. Our purpose is twofold:

1. We are conducting experiments, especially in the area of England, to determine if our efforts can affect the planet's ability to produce greater paramagnetic vortexes that will support more plant life.
2. We are trying to produce a "raised harmonics condition" for the planet, through the selected shapes we choose to create on the planet's surface.

If one begins to study the Pythagorean concept of the Music of the Spheres, one understands that all is one within the universe, and that all of creation is sound energy. In fact, all reality manifested in the physical world is thought energy, solidified through sound vibrations. All cosmic forces (which one might view as the macrocosm, depending upon one's perception of creation) are contained within the microcosm. While the microcosm is the individual and the electron that supports each atom within the human body, this microcosm can also be viewed as the Earth. We view the present crises on Earth as having resulted from separated attitudes which have created thought patterns that have removed the planet from its natural state of being "one" with the universe and all universes contained within. Therefore, our work and experiments are conducted to restore this condition, and unite your world with the Unified Field that supports life.

In reality, the Earth and its inhabitants are never separate from the Unified Field, because this force contains all intelligence and supports all life as "one". What has been created on Earth, however, through experimentation, technology and research, is a situation that has tampered with the laws of "the One" and created conditions that have separated the parts. This situation has caused "dis-ease", which to us means "out of harmony". Out of harmony means that one is out of the harmonics with the sound frequencies that support the Unified Field. The harmonics come from Light and sound frequencies, which create all life and existence as you know it to be.

Our work with the Crop Circles is conducted with the intent to bring the harmonics back into balance. We choose the area near Stonehenge, because this geographical area is one of the primary vortexes that affects the entire world. When one studies ley-lines and grid-lines and learns of the frequency patterns contained within these mini-vortexes, one realizes there are vortexes that contain several frequency points which have the capacity to affect the entire planet more powerfully than other points of entrance. Stonehenge and its surrounding area is such a location. From the beginning of time, we have known where the vortexes are that support the highest energies for distributing and balancing electromagnetic currents within the planet. That is why sacred structures appear all over the world and why they have been constructed for centuries. Structures like pyramids, round towers, domes, pillars and geodesic complexities are strategically placed to assure the balance of paramagnetic forces. Unfortunately, this condition has changed on the beloved Terra in the last 100 years of your Earth time. Presently, the Earth's currents are not balanced, and because they are not, there are many undesirable occurrences that have resulted, causing much pain and suffering. We have heard your cries for assistance and now offer help to those who wish for us to provide a way in which the Earth might redeem itself and lift itself out of its dilemma.

Our work in the area of England is essential for the planet, if the inhabitants of Earth wish to move beyond the year 2012. This is so. Our work with symbols and radionic experiments provides needed frequencies to change the electromagnetic conditions of your world. Each shape we use on the planet's surface carries with it a unique vibration or harmonic. Everything in creation has its own vibration and harmonic -- nothing is duplicated. That is one of the primary keys of creation. Know this to be true and you will have mastered half of the curriculum of Earth and the world in which you reside.

The patterns we bring to the world are those which contain the harmonics and vibrations lacking on Earth. These patterns are also the strongest symbols known for producing the resonance needed to penetrate Earth's core and to radiate the appropriate levels of electromagnetic energies to other areas of the planet. The language through the symbols is nothing other than the language of life. You will also find that the pattern of placement of these symbols correlates with the Heavens. This must be so, for the macrocosm is always contained within the microcosm.

The Tribunal Council of the Galactic Command thanks you for this opportunity to address your questions of concern. We look forward to another moment of your time, when we might converse again.

Good day in the Light of Our Most Radiant One.

I AM Soltec. Adonai.[29]

[29]*Majestic Raise*, Oct/Nov/Dec 1996.
Transmission received by Dr. Norma Milanovich, Albuquerque, NM, 1996.
Copyright at Athena Leadership Center.

PART THREE

CODES IN NEW JERUSALEM

Having received the Grail *water*, our fellow Knights in America immediately resumed their mission.

Much work was carried out across the country. The following are reports of some of the group work that was undertaken.

Photo by Clare Lincoln

THE HOLY GRAIL CODES
ARE TRANSFERRED TO AMERICA

The Coded Grail *water* was transferred by Sandy, who had personally flown to the USA, ensuring that it bypassed the airport security X-ray mechanism, to be delivered safely to its next seven-month cycle in America. We were now ready to fulfil our responsibility, wherever it took us. Our seven-month time frame in America was August, 1998 through February, 1999.

Kate, in Hollywood, California, was given the sacred responsibility of the keeper of the Codes for America. In order that the work be dispersed throughout Canada and the USA, she initially spent time bottling and mailing a small amount of the *water* to each Knight from both countries who had taken part in the France Journey. Although work was done by all of us throughout both countries the following reports concentrate on the American South-West. As it turns out, this is not by accident, since the larger hand of Spirit orchestrates all. The sacred sites and vortices in California, Arizona and Colorado seemed to mirror a pattern of preparatory work needed for a future group, which would journey in May, 2001 to the American South-West to open a major portal and anchor energies for the building of the **Temple of Love and Light**.

These are our stories.

(Lynne)

The American South-West

Yellowstone

OREGON

Boise   Jackson

Mount Shasta

Sacramento   Salt Lake City

San Francisco   Yosemite   Arches   Bever Creek

Denver

CALIFORNIA   Death Valley   Grand Canyon   Lake Powell   **COLORADO**

Mount Blanca

Los Angeles   Las Vegas   Santa Fe

Anaheim   Sedona

Catalina Island   Palm Springs   Joshua Tree   Albuquerque

Phoenix   **NEW MEXICO**

ARIZONA

Tucson   Carlsbad

El Paso

PACIFIC OCEAN   San Antonio

Cabo San Lucas

KAUAI   Lihue
Walmea
OAHU   Waikiki   Kapalua
Honolulu   Kaanapali   MAUI
Lanaina
Hilo

HAWAIIAN ISLANDS   Kona   HAWAII

102

JOURNEY TO AVALON
- Beloved Camelot -

(Catalina Island off the Coast of California - 12.9.1998)

The Journey to Avalon was absolutely amazing. There were seven of us Knights.

The number seven represents the spiritual forces, as seen in all the ritualistic orders, as well as in the forces of nature and those that react to the sensual forces of man. This is according to Edgar Cayce, who also said that seven usually represents a mystical relationship of completion. It is easy to see how everything was perfectly set for what was to happen -- what was to be co-created with the universe in this magical land that certainly holds the vibrational frequency of our **Camelot**. You need only to step foot in the city to feel the utopia of that not-so-distant place.

We were smiling with joy as we neared the dock at Avalon when a couple of dolphins greeted us. It was as if we had travelled across the moat, leaving the old world behind us. And we truly did...entering the "**Castle of Camelot**" and hence the "Ninth Dimension" once more on our sacred mission with the Codes in our possession, and in our BEing.

Lynne had been led to prepare some decrees inspired by the France Journey. The tone was truly set etherically and energetically by Lynne and the Masters. We each read the decrees silently along the way, remembering the truths and our mission.

As we walked off the boat we noticed a sign that announced St. Catherine's Church. We laughed, since there were two Kathryns present.

We knew we had to go there, as I read the decree from "The Church of Love" on Lynne's hand-out! Would that church symbolize the Cathars' proclamation? Catherine is from the same root name as Cathar, and they both mean "pure". Could we raise up its energy truly to be "The Church of Love" the Cathars decreed?

We walked down the street looking for clues to the location of this church that carried our name. A horse and carriage came by with a bride and groom and we congratulated them. The horse-drawn carriage had gone to the right and we wondered if we should follow. It seemed logical that they would go towards a church. We continued towards it.

The church was charming. We were at the side door. I knew all at once that we were to pour the Codes into the holy water designated for the people to use to anoint themselves.

I went in and towards the back. I absorbed the energy, which was lovely. There were two statues of female saints, St. Therese of the Child Jesus, and, of course, St. Catherine of Alexandria. I read the inscription of St. Therese and it was truly wonderful. Then, the words under St. Catherine took my breath away and brought warm tears to my eyes.

One of our desires had been to know the historical significance of Catalina Island. EVERYTHING was here. Everything...and much more than we had ever expected. I transcribed St. Catherine's legacy:

> St. Catherine of Alexandria was martyred, according to her
> legend, in Egypt around 300 A.D. Her executioners tried to use
> a spiked wheel, which has since become her identifying symbol.

The wheel broke, however, and she was killed by a sword.

She was believed to be the wisest woman in Alexandria, which was the intellectual capital of the Mediterranean world at that time. She is often shown with a book to symbolize her great wisdom and knowledge. She is the patroness of philosophers, secretaries, millers and women seeking a husband. From the time of the crusades in the 1100's to the Protestant Reformation in 1500, she was one of Europe's most popular saints and the subject of many great artists of that period.

St. Joan of Arc claimed to have been guided by her. She is one of the most venerated saints of the Greek Orthodox Catholic Church. Her body is entombed in the monastery at the foot of Mount Sinai in the Egyptian desert.

This island was first sighted by Captain Sebastian Viscaino on November 25, 1602 and was named "Santa Catalina" in her honor.

Well, we knew we were in the right place! The rest of our group began to wander in and we realized that the wedding was nearing its time. We had to work fast now. We guided the others to read St. Catherine's inscription and they were all amazed. Candy and I poured some of the Codes into the huge bowl, which was situated in the middle of the entrance at the back of the church. It was placed on a stand over three feet high and actually resembled a gigantic Holy Grail!

People were approaching the church now in preparation for the wedding ceremony. We gathered around the Holy Grail and held hands in a silent meditation. It was so powerful and so loving.

We all felt/saw the white Light in the centre going through the holy water. We were filled with *Love, Wisdom and Power*.

The fact that the wedding was going on was so perfect -- the integration of the feminine and masculine energies right before our very eyes, and all part of our own ceremony. It was the day of the Half Moon, which according to Master Kuthumi is the most powerful time of the merging of these two energies within us. Our ceremony was silent. It had to be energetically and vibrationally performed.

We anointed ourselves with the totally renewed holy water and left the church, which would witness the joining of woman and man.

We then walked back along the coast, pouring some of the Codes into the Pacific Ocean at a beautiful point with high rocks that housed lots of stately pelicans. We saw the whole Pacific Ocean, the whole planet "Coded".

We had dinner together and then slowly walked towards the boat for our departure home.

A private room behind the captain awaited us on board and we celebrated with a sip of champagne. The toast was, of course, "All for One and One for All".

(Kate)

© 1985-2002 AD Nanette Crist Johnson   Cabala Revealed (Holy Couple)

THE CHURCH OF LOVE

The last of the Cathars was burnt by the Inquisition of the Roman Catholic Church at Montségur, Languedoc, France in 1244, but they left this prophecy:
That the Church of Love would be proclaimed in 1986.

It has no fabric, only understanding.

It has no membership, save those who know they belong.

It has no rivals, because it is non-competitive.

It has no ambition, because it only seeks to serve.

It knows of no boundaries, for nationalisms are unloving.

It is not of itself, because it seeks to enrich all groups and
    religions.

It acknowledges all great teachers of all the ages who have
    shown the Truth of Love.

Those who participate practise the Truth of Love in all their
    daily being.

There is no walk of life or nationality that is a barrier.

Those who are, know.

It seeks not to teach, but to be and, by being, enrich.

It recognizes the collectivity of all humanity and that we are all
    one with the One.

It recognizes that the way we are may be the way of those
    around us, because we are that way.

It recognizes the whole planet as a Being of which we are a part.

It recognizes that the time has come for the supreme
    transmutation, the ultimate alchemical act, the conscious
    change of the ego into a voluntary return to the whole.

It does not proclaim itself with a loud voice, but in the subtle
    realms of loving.

It salutes all those in the past who have blazoned the path, but
    paid the price.

It admits of no hierarchy or structure, for no one is greater than
    another.

Its members shall know each other by their deeds and being and
    their eyes and by no other outward sign save the fraternal
    embrace.

Each one will dedicate his or her life to the silent loving of their
    neighbour and environment and the planet, whilst carrying
    out their daily task, however exalted or humble.

It recognizes the supremacy of the great idea, which may only
    be accomplished if the human race practises the supremacy
    of Love.

It has no rewards to offer, either here or in the hereafter, save
  that of the ineffable joy of being and loving.
Its members shall seek only to advance the cause of
  understanding, within whichever church, group or family
  they happen to be.
They shall do good by stealth and teach only by example.
They shall heal their neighbour, their community and our Planet.
They shall know no fear and feel no shame and their witness
  shall prevail over all odds.
It has no secrets, no arcanum, no initiation, save that of the true
  understanding of the power of Love and that, if we want it to
  be so, the world will change, but only if we change ourselves
  first.

All Those Who Belong, Belong,
That Is the Church of Love.

Printed through the courtesy of Fountain International (UK).

MOUNT BLANCA

- Pilgrimage to an Etheric Retreat -

(Sangre de Cristo Range, Colorado - 23/24.9.1998)

I left early in the morning from Denver, with a clear, Colorado blue sky and a significant tail wind blowing me south down the road. As I approached the Blanca Massif over four hours later that morning, the summit was enveloped in a thick blanket of clouds -- a sure sign that council was being held at that etheric retreat and plans were being made for our arrival. I knew this scenario well, as I had lived in the area and seen this site often during my tenure in the Valley of the Blood of Christ Mountains. I turned west to Alamosa and met my compatriots Sonora and Charlene at their motel room, where we ate, then did a preparatory meditation for our ascent and ceremony on the slopes of Blanca. Sonora and I had been there before for the 12:12 portal opening in 1994. We knew only to expect the unexpected and allow Spirit to lead the way.

As we drove east towards the mountain and the gate leading up to the Falls, the summit suddenly cleared, and Blanca, in all of its splendour, showed itself. The way had been made clear for us, and there, where it had always been, was the gate and dirt road leading up to the Falls! We knew instinctively that it would appear for us as soon as I committed to this Journey and ceremony...and so it was!

The wind blew us up the steep switch-back. As we neared the parking lot, Sonora started relaying the messages and guidance she was receiving for the specifics of the ceremonial site. We were to follow the main path to the Falls, then find our own way -- no small task on this steep, rugged, cactus-covered mountainside! But as we started out, Sonora was a bulldog and Charlene and I dutifully followed, knowing that guidance would take us to the perfect spot. Sonora told us that this spot would have almost a 360-degree vista. Indeed, in what seemed like a small eternity, we found a wind-swept spot, overlooking the entire Valley! It was breathtaking! As we started the ceremony, the wind howled around us, as if to accentuate the point of the ceremony itself: Out with the Old; In with the New. As we finally uttered the words "So Be It and So It Is!", the wind suddenly stopped and an eerie calm surrounded us. We stood in a triangle, held hands, placed stones, specially coded crystals from Kentucky and the Coded *water* in our centre, blessed it, and sent that blessing out into the universe, willing it to return a thousand-fold. With that, we simply stood on that sacred spot and absorbed the spectacular vista and the magnificent energy we had co-created with Spirit and the mountain.

We eventually made our way back to the Falls and I performed a ceremony and poured some of the Grail *water* in the stream, to be whisked down the mountain into the San Luis Valley below. That Valley will certainly never be the same!

We celebrated our wonderful day by dining at an Alamosa restaurant and toasting our success...with our guides in attendance!

As I drove back to Denver the next morning, I noticed that the sky was somehow bluer than before, that the Fall colour was somehow more vibrant than I had noticed on the way down. Details I had not noticed suddenly popped out. The journey home went by in a flash. Such are the rewards when one fulfils his/her commitments made between lifetimes. What a reward this has been for me!

Kodoish, Kodoish, Kodoish Adonai Tsebayoth.

"So Be It, and So It Is!"

(Lynne)

THE HEART JOURNEY OF SELF DISCOVERY

(Joshua Tree National Park, California - 25/28.9.1998)

Christine from England, who spent several months in the USA working on the Codes with us, and Richard joined me for four glorious days on a spiritual retreat at Joshua Tree National Park and the surrounding vicinity. It is very close to the Palm Springs area here in California. And as Ron Wescott, our spiritual leader, said, within the sacred heart of Mother Earth sleeps the Galactic ancient wisdom of many civilizations. In this National Forest one can experience the heart Journey of self-discovery.

We all experienced incredible personal initiations while Coding the entire area. We hiked high into the mountains, reaching sacred sites to which our leader had been guided to take us. We meditated in the Queen's and King's Chamber, and we climbed the key mount at Pyramid Mountain. We chanted sacred mantras on top of Crystal Mountain while looking for spaceships from Sirius, Arcturus and the Pleiades. We prayed at Giant Rock (the world's largest free-standing boulder) while scanning the Milky Way and Orion's Stargate.

The highlight was staying in the Integratron, which is a dome-shaped building said to be a space of healing and eternal life. It is built on sacred grid-lines corresponding to the Great Pyramid at Giza, and the vibration in there is simply amazing. When you stand in the exact centre of the structure and speak or chant, it feels as if the sound is coming from directly within you. You must experience it personally to feel the exhilaration of the vibrations that seem to be resounding and coming from the innermost recesses of your Being.

One of the facilitators brought a prototype of the Chartres Cathedral Labyrinth! We got to walk it this time, and what a phenomenal experience that was. It was like a Journey through life itself. On the route to the centre we experienced everything from joy and love of BEing to issues of doubts and fear. When each of us arrived in the centre, a halo representing sacred geometry (a twelve-pointed star) was placed on our head as the group chanted "hallelujah" to the most beautiful music in praise of our completion. It was like being Home!

When I saw the Chartres Labyrinth on the itinerary, I knew I had to take the Codes there! I placed our sacred version of the Holy Grail right in the centre of the labyrinth, where the true essence of *Love, Wisdom and Power* was sent out through our planet into the universe.

(Kate)

The Labyrinth of Chartres

Printed through the courtesy of RILKO Books.

WALKING THE SACRED RINGS

(Death Valley, California - 4.10.1998)

Death Valley was the next site. Rudy and I accompanied a few of our close spiritual friends to this place to walk the Sacred Rings. These are created for the same reason as the Crop Circles. They are circular mounds about four feet in diameter made by the elemental kingdom, the elves and fairies, to harmonize our Earth. They are located in very remote areas where it is so quiet that you can hear the breath of the planet. As we walked along, Coding them, we felt the beautiful, harmonious energies of love and peace. Then we found a little labyrinth that they had created, where we could just envision the fairies all joyously dancing around a huge fire.

As the sun began to set against the desert mountains, colouring the sky with peaches, pinks and violets, we reached a little valley, where I was certain there was a spaceship. I could feel it in the air. I was compelled to go down to get closer, and was relieved when the group decided to descend. When we got into the valley, I noticed quite a large hill, and I knew the spaceship was hovering directly above it. So I left the group and climbed up. Ascending the hill, I could feel intense energies almost pounding on me. The ground was charred white and crispy under my hiking boots. I adjusted my breathing to take in the frequencies that appeared to be coming from above me. I positioned myself exactly in the centre of the top of the hill, for that was where I knew the spaceship was beaming down its Light. I had to squat because it was "raining" on me so intensely. I enjoyed the exchange and knew it to be powerful and positive.

After some time, I saw the group leaving and decided to follow them. Besides, I don't think I could have taken much more. As I walked up the slope, I turned and looked at the hill where I had been. I said in my mind, "I know you are there. Let me see you. Come on, it won't hurt. Just let me see a glimpse." I continued to catch up to my friends, and the sun was fast disappearing, the Light fading. Once more, I turned and looked at the site. And what did I behold? The spaceship! I saw it -- the classic saucer shape with a dome on top in the centre. It was the same diameter as the hill and was sitting above it about 30 feet. A part of me was slightly stunned, while another part felt that it was the most natural occurrence and nothing phenomenal at all. I laughed as the image melted into the final darkness from the setting sun. Putting my hands in my pockets for warmth, I realized that the Codes were in my pocket....

(Kate)

PRAISE TO MOUNT SHASTA

Guardian of Truth
Standing at the portal to other worlds of understanding.

Your radiance is a beacon to all who come
As travellers on the path of life.

Your purity shines and sparkles in your snow-capped summit
White crystallized water refracting the Light of Spirit.

Speaking to our hearts of who we truly are
Your magnificence and power holds
The Majesty of our Divine Being.

(Felicity, London, June 1999)

© Erich Ziller

MOUNT SHASTA
ROOT OF ALL BEGINNINGS
- Message from the Cosmic Ascended Masters -

Mount Shasta, the Base Chakra for the Earth, is considered by the Spiritual Hierarchy to be the corner-stone for this planet, and they elaborate on this as follows:

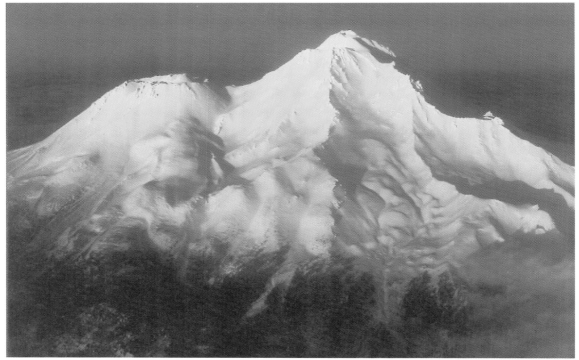

© CH2M Hill

It is the foundation of manifestation, it is in essence the navel point of the Earth, a point that was used at the beginning of time to be the original core from which all creation leapt forth. It was the first piece of the Earth to be made manifest, from which all manifestation spread forth and formed the Earth. It was the first piece of the planet that was used to harbour life and it was always the foundation upon which different forms of manifestation would first find existence on the planet.

It has been used, then, time and time again as the blank canvas upon which God has painted.

It was the original material, the original medium, the original conduit, the original base from which all began.

It is close to the Masters, because it is still used today as a point of emanation through which vibration can be translated into manifestation here upon the physical form and planet.

It is essential, then, for it forms the feet upon which all else is balanced and stored. It is the final part of the ladder that allows communication to be so beneficially communicated to all those upon the Earth who would have heart and mind to hear it. It is a reception point, like a lightning conductor or a tuning fork that absorbs sound or lightning energy and allows the distribution of this frequency and force to occur throughout the world.

It is a special point that exists in many dimensions simultaneously in many forms. It is a point of convergence, a point of alignment and a point of manifestation.[30]

[30]Channelled by Edwin Courtenay, London, 16.8.1999.

CLOSE ENCOUNTER WITH THE ASCENDED MASTERS

- Heights of Mount Shasta -

(California - 16/17.10.1998)

© Armando de Melo

I had embraced this sparkling crystalline temple twice over the years from an aeroplane, in total amazement. My heart shifted each time I saw it and I remained spellbound. How I had longed to go to it some day....

Well, that day arrived. Christine and I drove to Sacramento to meet Vera, who lovingly hosted us, and then the three of us continued on to the most magical place I have experienced yet on this beloved planet.

The first sight of it blew us away. It was breathtaking. Shasta took us tenderly into her arms and enchanted us beyond any expectations we could have entertained. The feeling of the Ascended Masters is overwhelming. We felt so close to their etheric retreat.

Finally, we were ascending along the winding roads lined with tall, protective evergreens. The snow-capped magical mountain changed each moment as we approached it, as if it were moving and alive. Was it reacting to us? And what pristine air! I wanted to fill my lungs with it -- every cell in my body felt the energy of such a pure atmosphere. It felt as if I were taking in the Breath of God.

We stopped at the highest peak that our car could ascend and prepared to climb up a little. Vera, Christine and I began to hike up together. It was lovely, and the higher we got, the more sublime it felt. Vera decided to stay at a certain point and Christine and I felt like continuing. We hiked another hour or so, found some snow to quench our thirst and rested in a sunny, rocky area. We silently separated to find places to meditate and just be.

Then Christine decided to stay behind, while I was feeling a strong power pulling me towards the summit, which was beginning to resemble the three-pointed Crown of **Camelot**.

Pretty soon I identified the quickest route to make my way up. I saw a ridge, like a plateau. It seemed to be the moat leading into **Camelot**. When I walked it, I would leave the "old world" behind and enter into a new magical existence. And after that, I saw that I could go right up towards the top, as high as I wanted to.

As I eventually crossed the plateau, I saw two hawks in the distance and beckoned them to me. I said, "Come fly over me and show me how beautiful you are." Within seconds, as if they heard my call, they were flying low over my head hawking away, leading me on. They flew directly to the top, the Crown of Shasta, the Crown of **Camelot**.

Now, the fact that I was going to the peak of Shasta was slightly alarming, since it was late afternoon in October. The sun would be setting soon. NO problem, Soltec would take care of the time. I HAD to go to the top. The climbing became difficult and then brutal. I was going straight up and traversing rocks of all sizes, and some of these were not stable. Checking my watch occasionally and watching the sun, I continued, enjoying the absolutely phenomenal view that was appearing before my eyes.

I had already decided that the only way to return was to slide down on the deep snow drifts, which were like mini-glaciers. This was not only safer, but was going to be essential, since I would need to conserve time. The sun was already descending in the amber western sky. I continuously checked my inner guidance for instruction, while sending messages to Vera and Christine that I was all right. I knew they would be wondering. It had been hours since I left them with no idea that I would be climbing to the top of Mount Shasta!

The climbing became so intense that I had to concentrate only on the next step so I would not panic. I had to rest at every move -- it was so strenuous.

I knew why I had to do this, not just for my own personal Journey (though that was indeed significant), but for all of us. I climbed Shasta for the Codes, for what they represented. I was Coding Shasta.... When I hit a large mass of snow, I poured the Codes over it, knowing the essence would come forth in Spring, bringing rebirth and regeneration.

I was about 100 to 150 feet from the summit as I hugged a solid rock for safety from the howling winds that occasionally swept around me. In stillness I looked at the incredible view I now had the blessed gift of seeing. I made myself concentrate -- not only on the visuals, but on the feeling of what it was like to be so high and close to God. I never wanted to forget it. The remembrance still brings tears of joy to my heart. I believe it always will. I am to remain forever an innocent witness and blessed recipient in awe of God's love.

As I basked in the Oneness, I heard a voice inside me say "Well done, Daughter." I felt the presence of all the Masters -- Sananda, St. Germain, Maitreya, Yogananda, Quan Yin, Buddha, and more. It was a glorious and triumphant moment, but I could not celebrate for too long.

In 3-D reality, it was five o'clock and the sun was setting rapidly. I was amazed that I had almost reached the summit in such a short time. And now, I had to descend fast or else I would be hiking down a treacherous rocky slope in the dark. I wanted to continue up to the crown, to stay up there -- forever -- but I knew that it would have to be another time and that I had completed my mission for now.

I tied my colourful ski jacket around my waist, making sure the Codes were safely tucked away inside my pocket. I used the jacket as a sled, sliding down the snowy drifts that resembled mini-glaciers. It was quite tricky, as I was travelling very fast at times on the steep slope, but after a few bumps, I learned to manoeuvre myself safely down.

Eventually I returned to the plateau leading out of **Camelot** and into the world below where I had come from. I prayed for the time I needed to return safely, and felt as if the pending darkness were racing with me.

Soon I was hiking down the final part of the trail in darkness. I envisioned where I felt I was to go and knew it could not be much further. I still sent the message that I was safe to Vera and Christine below. But I began to notice that the trail felt a little different. Then I remembered a fork a way back. I had taken the wrong trail. Being on a foreign trail was not comfortable. So I decided to send a message to Vera and Christine to "come get me." I then envisioned them coming with a flashlight. It could not have been more than three minutes when I felt Christine's vibration. I called out her name, and instantly a flashlight appeared about a hundred feet from me. That was one of my quickest manifestations to date!

I literally limped to the car. Yes, I had been brave, but only by the Grace of God had I been able to pull it off. I lovingly felt the Codes in my pocket once more as we drove down that phenomenal mountain.

The following day, before we left that gorgeous, crystal-capped mountain, Vera, Christine and I went to Panther Meadow, which is about a quarter of the way up. We meditated together with the Codes in this sacred meadow. Then Vera asked for a sign, and as we walked back to the car Christine saw it in the sky. It was a colourful rainbow prism around the dazzling sun. What an awesome gift for a glorious Journey.

(Kate)

THE LOVE DOLPHINS HOLD FOR HUMANITY

Dolphins have been with us since the beginning of time. They carry the Lemurian energy -- the original God force. These beings of love, joy and laughter are here with their purity to assist us in our evolution.

© Roger Bishop

SWIMMING WITH DOLPHINS
- Transformation with Joy -

(Kona, Hawaii)

About a year ago I started to tune into the Dolphin energy. And before I knew it, I was compelled to plan a Journey with Candy and two other spiritual friends to swim with these amazing creatures of joy. For Thanksgiving week we met in Kona, Hawaii, on the Big Island to join Joan Ocean for one of the most incredible and transforming Journeys of our lives. I took the Codes to give to the Dolphins.

On our first day out we immediately met up with a Humpback Whale. This huge, loving creature was magnificent and circled our boat, spouting away. What a gift this was, especially since it was the first sighting of a Whale in that area that year! He came to greet us. We soon discovered a pod of Spinner Dolphins dancing up out of the water joyously. They seemed to like entertaining us humans and checked us out with watchful, loving eyes. At my first sight of about six of them, swimming in unison gracefully over the crystal clear blue water, tears ran streaming down my face, in ecstasy to be reunited with my friends, from where and when I knew not exactly. It did not matter. We knew each other and were together again.

As I was standing on the front tip of the catamaran watching the Spinners playfully swim alongside of the boat, one came directly in front -- so close I could have bent down and touched him. I was deeply drawn to him and easily tuned into his energy. It seemed as if he were speaking to me in those enticing, high-frequency, melodious notes. Then he started to "jabber" away with all kinds of tones. It seemed as if he were sending out thought vibrations that I understood! I was moved beyond description by this amazing communication, which I knew was just for me. When I told Joan about it later, she asked me what the Dolphin had said to me and for the first time I translated the telepathic thoughts into words. He said that he knew I had brought the gift of the Codes and that he would receive them with honour. Then he said that he would swim beside me the following day. Well, I just took it for granted that this was the truth and simply let it go. We stopped the boat and got in the water to interact with the Dolphins. But they promptly disappeared. We soon found them again and again. And every time we would get in the water they would be nowhere to be found. Undaunted, we agreed at meditation that evening that they were making us stretch ourselves to be with them on higher realms first, and we had no doubt that we would have our Dolphin encounters soon enough. They were also checking out our energies as a group -- there were 12 of us, including Joan and her co-facilitator.

The next day we found the same group of Dolphins again. They were a little more interactive, and we could feel that they were ready to play. They were sonaring us a lot now, sending out the vibrations from their Third Eyes, aligning our chakras and working on our energy fields. The sounds were phenomenally healing.

We jumped in to join our long-lost friends. I don't quite know how it happened, but all of a sudden I had a Dolphin on each side of me and one directly in front. I could have just reached out on either side and easily touched them, they were that close to my body. How I could swim that fast to keep up with them, I had no idea. Maybe they graciously slowed down or just "took" me with them. I was a princess, a Goddess in a Dolphin Chariot. I felt the most incredible feeling of joy and Oneness in their precious vehicle of love and harmony. I was one of them. They accepted me and honoured me. I realized in those moments that the Dolphin who had communicated with me the day before was on my left.

The final day of our swim we entered a sacred bay and were joined by four different pods -- over three hundred Dolphins! Joan said they came to meet us. Everywhere we looked there were Dolphins, swimming, spinning and making love. It was mating season and some had already given birth to darling little Dolphins who were learning the art of spinning up out of the water to take a look at their earthly dimension above, AND to check us out and receive our laughter and applause. The sonaring was unbelievable. I stayed in the water for four hours with them, wanting to BE them, to become one with them and stay with them forever.

I poured the *sacred water* into the ocean and they took the Codes into their energy. They are the Holy Grail Codes -- *Love, Wisdom, Power and Oneness.* The only other Journey that has transformed me as much was the one to France. Later that evening my ear drums were so sensitive that I don't think I could have handled another high-pitch frequency. I needed to integrate the awesome adventures and alignments into all of my bodies, especially energetically.

After I returned home, I found myself telling people that if I had stayed one more day, I surely would have shape-shifted into a Dolphin and stayed. I would tell them the story of the Dolphin Chariot, wondering how it could have possibly happened that I could swim fast enough to keep up with them. Then I "happened" to read a book about shape-shifting by John Perkins, who interacts with the shamans of the world.

I kept hearing myself share this story over and over. Then, miraculously one day, it suddenly and magically occurred to me that I actually HAD shape-shifted into a Dolphin in those moments. My feelings were confirmed, and although my human mind finds this too awesome to accept, there is a part of me that knows it is what happened.

All our oceans and Dolphins and Whales are now Coded, my Dear Friends of the Round Table. I was guided to do this, and there was no force, fear or doubt that could have kept me from it, even though it was logistically and feasibly a difficult trip to make.

(Kate)

JOURNEY TO DISNEYLAND
- Transformation in the Magic Kingdom -

(Anaheim, California - 26.11.1998)

About three weeks before my scheduled departure from Denver to the Los Angeles area, I received a "visit". The "energy" was familiar, yet unfamiliar. When I asked who this was, an inner vision manifested. To my amazement and delight, it was Walt Disney himself! I could hardly believe what I was seeing. He had come as the result of a question I had asked: "How can I assist the Project you started here on Earth in the form of cartoon animation and, later, The Magic Kingdom -- Disneyland?" He said, "Yes, Lynne, you can help." What followed were brief inner vision scenarios, which involved going to Disneyland and doing something (I did not know exactly what at that time) to clear the misplaced energy of the park itself and insert an upgraded Full-Light Spectrum Containment Field, *which is another way of expressing the concept of "perfect source, perfect reflection". The full-light spectrum field is, of course, Source/God.* Wow! A tall order to fill.

During the next three weeks, Ascended Master Walt was with me frequently, feeding my inner vision with images, and showing me that there was a pattern and cosmic layout to his original theme park. I met with others who helped me understand the energetic layout of the park, what it meant and how I could use it to upgrade the energy. Actually, it is more accurate to say that I would be assisting Ascended Master Walt and his Group to restore the park to its original energetic intent. I called my good friend, Richard, who gladly consented to accompany me. We determined that our mere physical presence, along with the Grail-Coded *water,* and our pure intent would be enough to change the energy. Now, this was quite a realization, considering the volume of people flowing through that site every day of the year! This just goes to prove that each one of us can make a difference.

Since the park itself is based on a configuration like a wagon wheel, with a centre and spokes radiating out from that centre, we made for the centre of the park, which just happens to be Sleeping Beauty's Castle. We found a lovely little waterfall, complete with Snow White and the Seven Dwarves around it. I poured the Coded *water* in the Falls and we both stood silently for about five minutes or so, then looked up at each other and said "Well, guess that's it. We are done." We had both gotten the guidance simultaneously. It seemed...well, too simple. Yet, Spirit tells us that's the way it is meant to be.

I believe that Sleeping Beauty represents the unawakened Creator Within. And the Castle is the fortress, protecting that unawakened Creative potential. Our Grail-Coded *water* was the elixir to awaken that fully empowered Creator Within. Walt knew this, and the site plan of his "Magic Kingdom" reflected this with its sacred geometric layout. Sleeping Beauty has slumbered, waiting for the Prince (the Codes) to awaken her out of the Illusion (the Seven Dwarfs, as representatives of seven attributes of third-dimensional physical existence). The waterfall and Coded *water* represent Cosmic Consciousness, carrying the enlightened Codes of the universe. It is all there, and Walt knew it while we "slumbered". Yet, he also knew that anyone passing through the gates of his "Magic Kingdom" would be forever changed. And so it is!

Richard and I had a grand day. So much had changed since I was last there. However, the "spirit" in which Walt Disney created his beloved Kingdom has never left. We just assisted him in restoring it to its original intent.

Ascended Master Walt still "looks" in on me from time to time, reminding me that, once one steps up to the platform of Light, one can never go back! His wry, mischievous smile and gentle energy are there, urging me to see the connectedness in all sentient consciousness. He says it is why he used "the rodent" (that is what he calls Mickey). A most unlikely Emissary to humanity, bridging the gap between Humanity and the Animal Kingdom.

Thank you, Ascended Master Walt!

Kodoish, Kodoish, Kodoish Adonai Tsebayoth.

So Be It, and So It Is!

(Lynne)

EXPERIENCING POWERFUL
VORTEX ENERGIES

(Sedona, Arizona)

Christine and I met in Phoenix with plans to drive to Sedona with the Codes the day after Christmas. We proceeded to Code the area around Phoenix, especially Superstition Mountain, Red Mountain and the Mormon Church, where we saw an amazing colourful Light display. We put the *holy water* everywhere, and on Christmas Day meditated for peace near Red Mountain. The following day we left for our final adventure together.

Sedona boasts the most accelerating energies I have ever experienced. There are four major vortexes, each offering unique energetic qualities of transformation. We Coded every one. Airport Vortex is peaceful and calming, Bell Rock is joyful and Lemurian, and Cathedral is very interdimensional and galactic. We hiked them all and sprinkled the Codes everywhere. We also went to the Chapel, which is built right into the red rock mountain. There is an interdimensional portal there to the time of Jesus when he was a baby. Across from the Chapel is a natural rock formation of the Mother and Child which exudes feminine nurturing energy. And high up on the mountain above the Chapel is a natural eagle's head, quietly watching over us. It is so obvious with its perfectly carved face in the red rock. Pure unconditional love envelops the site. We poured the *sacred water* in the bowl at the entrance, so that all who dip into it to bless themselves will be Coded. We also Coded Oak Creek, which seems to carry the life force of the entire area.

Then we went to Boynton Canyon, the fourth vortex. As we approached the enchanting energies, two red-tipped hawks flew over the car, leading the way into the canyon. They were so low that we could easily see their red markings. We knew we were in for a wonderful adventure now.

We hiked up in silence towards the auspicious Kachina rock which oversees the valley quite protectively. It was like a nurturing mother inviting you up into her bosom. I followed its call, leaving Christine to meditate in the glorious sunlight, which created the most delicious colours, multi-shades of orange and red mixed with sparkling tones of green. I knew from my many previous visits that there was a cave at the back of the foundation of the Kachina rock. And I knew I was to take the Codes there. I always ended up in this cave, whenever I was drawn to Sedona. The view is awesome from any angle, and I immediately experienced a feeling of gratitude as I reached the bottom of the gigantic monument. I was thankful for the opportunity of working with the Codes, for Christine for being there with me and for the beloved Journey to France that began a whole new adventure for me. I was grateful for my family, whom I held in my heart during that meditation, and for all my spiritual friends -- for you also are my family. I was grateful for life itself. I sprinkled the Codes in the cave and burnt some sage in honour of this spectacular day. I knew we were serving mankind in a way even greater than we knew, and in innocence I was in awe.

As Christine and I drove happily out of the canyon and onto the main road of Sedona, we saw one of the most extraordinary sights I have ever seen in my life. A flock of between 50 to 100 pure white doves (we could not count them, for there were too many!) flew in formation all around the luscious green and bright red rock mountains. They took our breath away, sparkling joyously in the sunlight. Then we remembered the symbol of the Dove on our France Journey, where it had all started exactly a year ago. We agreed that we must have done a good job, gazing incredulously at this glorious gift for us. What an incredible culmination of our Journey. It was a whirlwind two days, and we had covered every site we wanted to cover. I sometimes felt as if we *were* the vortexes, going around from place to place Coding everything. Maybe we were.

Sedona always supports you from the past, the future and the present to become the best that you can be. The challenge, when you are there, is to know this, understand it and allow it to exist.

Soon the precious Holy Grail Codes will be on their way to Australia. I wish Lesley and Jill, our two Australian Knights, a blessed incredible Journey with the Codes -- and a lot of fun!

(Kate)

PART FOUR

THE SPIRIT OF AUSTRALIA

The precious Holy Grail Codes were transferred by Richard, one of our American Knights. Australia comprises the largest Lemurian land mass on Earth. Its Spirit is presented by Lesley and Jill.

© Provided by Ayers Rock Management

©Axel Kayser

THE HOLY GRAIL CODES ARRIVE IN AUSTRALIA

Richard came to Australia with Norma on the sacred Journey "Awakening to the Dreamtime".

This Journey was to activate the last of the Lemurian Codes before the Millennial shift of consciousness on the planet. The occasion was to see the completion of the agreement which the Aboriginals had brought with them to Earth -- namely to carry the vision of the Fifth Dimension until the time came to release it to others who would "hold the dream of creation for tomorrow" -- hold "these geometric forms within...eventually carrying these Codes of Earth's future to other parts of the world". In this way the participating Lightworkers, destined to touch the inter-dimensional doorway of Uluru "at the cosmic moment of the New Millennium", were to "change the present probability of Earth's destiny and align it with the great plan of the Creator", in a Journey "designed to truly bring Heaven to Earth".[31]

Richard carried the Grail Codes to Uluru, and here the first Australian Grail ceremony was performed. There could not have been a more fitting place for the Codes to begin their Australian sojourn.

[31]*Spiritual Warriors to Carry Codes of Freedom for the World.*
  Transmission received by Dr. Norma Milanovich, Albuquerque, NM, 1998.
  Copyright at Athena Leadership Center.

In addition, Richard was to carry the Grail Codes throughout the "Dreamtime Journey" to Alice Springs, King's Canyon, the Olgas (Kata Tjuta), Tjapuki Aboriginal Culture Park, and the Outer Barrier Reef, Coding these areas also before posting the Grail *water* to us from Cairns.

Because we were not sure beforehand of the date of the Uluru activation and Richard's subsequent mailing of the Codes, a cosmi-time meditation was projected into the etheric on February 25, to be held there for the transference of the Keys and Codes to Australia through the crystalline electromagnetic Light grid on Earth.

(Lesley)

© Axel Kayser

THE UNVEILING OF THE MYSTERY OF ULURU

When We Open Our Hearts to the Silence
We Encounter the Mystery at the Centre of Australia.
Here One Can be Initiated into the Mystery.[32]

Elements of this mystery are revealed in *The Book of Love*, which was written under the guidance of Light Beings who are aspects of Sanat Kumara. It contains "factual" and channelled information on Uluru/The Rainbow Serpent and the traditional role of the Aboriginal People as custodians of the Earth. The following information is compiled from *The Book of Love*.

The Alcheringa Stone

The Book of Love tells of an ancient, very powerful sacred stone, the Alcheringa Stone, and its revelations. In Australian Aboriginal traditions the Tjuringa, the sacred stone, is apparently used to "connect and emphasize the 'God Energy' ".

The Alcheringa Stone was brought to Earth by Alcheringa, the Golden One, one of the "Star People", and entrusted to the Australian Aboriginals and their leader, Tjurunga. Many teachings were given to these "cherished ones", so that they would understand the existence of the Creator energy.

Maintaining deep respect within their hearts, these people have upheld their duty to look after and care for the Mother -- Earth -- through the ages, and have done so with great heart. Their work on the energy lines (these are sometimes referred to as "The Song Lines") has helped to maintain a balance of energies on and within the Earth.

The story of the Alcheringa Stone and its revelations is told by Valerie Barrow, who had temporary custodianship of the Stone and who has meditated with it.

To her, the Alcheringa Stone emanates a blue-white opalescent Light like that of a moonstone or feldspar. On a visit to the centre of Australia, she discovered that Uluru is made up partly of feldspar. She states that both the Alcheringa Stone and the sacred rock Uluru came from the same source -- the stars.

Alcheringa

Alcheringa, a representative of cosmic energies, is, as an aspect of Sanat Kumara, part of the Council of Light. He states that he is connected with all sacred sites on Earth and, in particular, the site known as Uluru, which is where he has his etheric residence. His name carries the connotations of "Messenger", "Dreamtime", and "Golden Age".

At the time of the Great Flood, ten thousand years ago, the original people of Australia called to God for help. A great being came in response, presenting himself as a black man. This being was Alcheringa.

---

[32]Quote from an A.B.C. Broadcast on the Australian Landscape as the Country of Silence.

He taught the people ceremonies using sound. He showed them how to perform a ceremony bringing in the Rainbow Serpent energy to help balance Earth's energy points.

We are told that "Uluru" means "Rainbow Serpent".

Following this initiation, the Aboriginal people have been the Earth Minders in both the Third and the Fourth Dimensions. Alcheringa speaks of them as the "Cherished Ones", for they have performed their duty unswervingly for thousands of years to help maintain a balance of energies on the Earth.

Uluru/Rainbow Serpent

Valerie learnt that Uluru, a huge monolith, came to Earth as an asteroid before man was present here. Five-eighths of the rock is submerged in the ground, but even so it is 546 metres high. It is four kilometres long, two to four kilometres wide and eight kilometres around the base.

© Provided by Ayers Rock Management

Uluru (Ayers Rock)

Partially quoting others, Valerie describes the area at Uluru as a Solar Plexus vibration raised to that of a Heart Centre, with energy lines like a nervous system radiating out to connect with all other sacred vortex points around the Earth.

She also describes the energies at Uluru (Ayers Rock) as "very male and powerful" and those at Kata Tjuta (The Olgas) as "gentle and female-feeling".

In information channelled from Alcheringa, we learn that "the energy from Uluru could be seen as the energy of 'the Lion' ".

Alcheringa speaks of an energy gateway coming through the Central Sun bringing in a "line" of influence, which historically has fostered creation activities and the lifting of consciousness of every being and form of life on Earth, including the consciousness of Earth itself. In speaking of this line of influence, known as the energy of "the Lion" (i.e. Sirius), Alcheringa adds, "...energy that has come through from another galaxy at another time filters into the Earth and comes through to various points at the surface.... Egypt is one of them.... Pyramids were built on many of those places. [The availability of this energy] allowed the 'Star People', who came to Earth at that time, to manifest and create."

Alcheringa relates that the "Star People" actually brought the rock Uluru to Earth for the purpose of bringing in this Creator energy of Universal Power and Intelligence, and "to help make changes upon the Earth so that it developed." This was before the advent of humanity. He adds that he himself, as an aspect of a "Star Being", has remained in the etheric to help with those [historical] changes and with the understandings to be filtered through to humanity, until a time that the Earth returns to a dimension which existed when the Rock first arrived here. That "formation" is now coming into being and will herald the New Age -- a time when all will operate within the Will of God and the Law of the Universe.

The Book of Love states,

> With the firing that took place with the Rock as it came into our atmosphere, it has flecks through it -- you can see it -- of semi-precious crystal or what looks like crystal or mica to the layman and really explains why, depending where the sun is, and what time of the year it is, the Rock glows in various different colours at times. It is quite wonderful the way it catches the Light.
>
> This energy is given off to touch Kata Tjuta (The Olgas) and affects that area also, because it is in direct alignment with Uluru.[33]

(Lesley)

---

[33]Excerpt from *The Book of Love* by Valerie Barrow. Published by the Diary Company Limited, Hong Kong, 1995. Distributors Alcheringa Books, PO Box 925, Bowral, NSW. Telephone (61) 02-48789304 Fax (61) 02-48789305.

A CALL OF FREEDOM

It is time to awaken to the dream of tomorrow,
Oh Sisters and Brothers of the world.

The currents of growth and abundance are strong,
and the winds of change are being felt
around the Earth.

The Mother breathes the new breath of freedom,
yet knows that it shall take several years
to experience this reality.

She cries aloud to the people of the world
to come forth now and walk with courage
and create the New Millennium.[34]

(Master Kuthumi)

[34]*Spiritual Warriors to Carry Codes of Freedom for the World.*
Transmission received by Dr. Norma Milanovich, Albuquerque, NM, 1998.
Copyright at Athena Leadership Center.

MOTHER EARTH...SHE CRIES

Softly she calls her people to continue to be guardians of their land.
Norma MacDonald

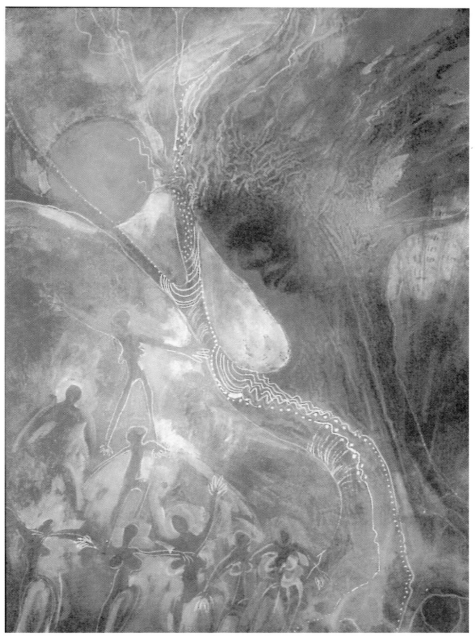

© Norma MacDonald

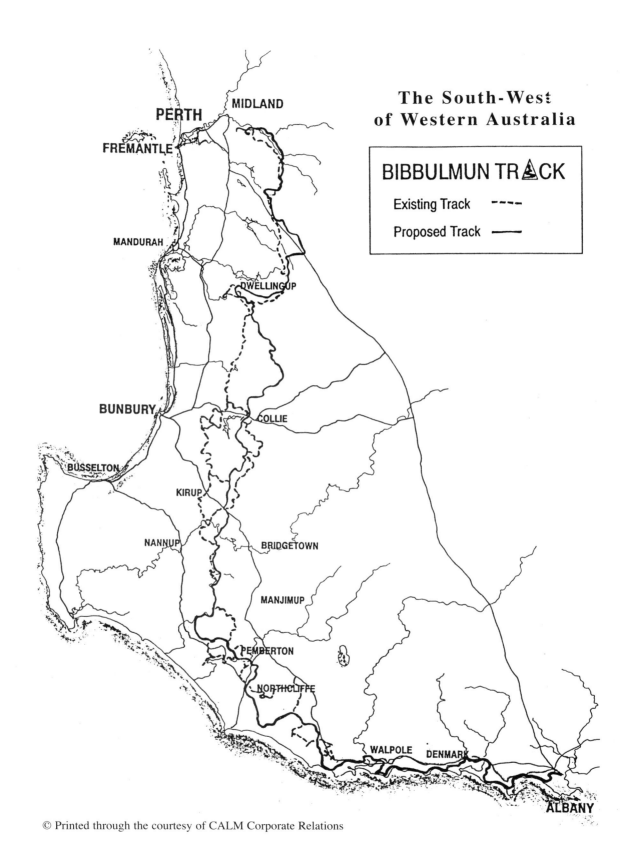

The South-West of Western Australia

BIBBULMUN TRACK

Existing Track - - - -

Proposed Track ——

PERTH

MIDLAND

FREMANTLE

MANDURAH

DWELLINGUP

BUNBURY

BUSSELTON

COLLIE

KIRUP

NANNUP

BRIDGETOWN

MANJIMUP

PEMBERTON

NORTHCLIFFE

WALPOLE

DENMARK

ALBANY

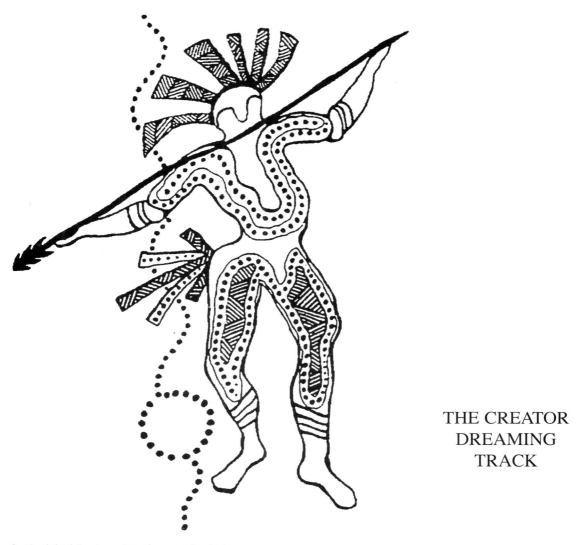

THE CREATOR
DREAMING
TRACK

Much knowledge of sacred places of power in Australia is held by the ancient Aboriginal peoples who have tended and nurtured such sites over the Millennia, bringing Spirit into matter.

Despite the fact that they might not be widely known, powerful vortexes do exist in a landscape that comprises the largest Lemurian land mass on Earth.

The Grail Codes work in Australia has had reference to Lemurian and more recent, but still ancient, Aboriginal influences, among others. The Light work always consisted of the implanting of the treasures of the Grail in the land. But beyond that, as it developed, I came to see it as (predominantly) two-fold -- the enactment of re-creation work, in the ancient Rainbow Serpent Creator Trails, for the Millennium; and the nurturing of energies of reconciliation to help in the current Reconciliation process between the indigenous creators/custodians and the more recent settlers.

In this context, in a recent channelling, the Masters describe

> the Holy Grail's energy as "a universal force that finds presence
> and pertinence in areas that are transcendent to its own cultural
> and religious reference" and state that "the energy can be seen,
> translated into other words, languages and religious metaphors
> throughout the world."[35]

In this way, most of the ceremonies have been carried out in the south-west of the country -- a region of tall Jarrah and Karri forests and bountiful water systems, pristine beaches framed by ageless rock formations and, near the coast, a network of ancient limestone caves.

The Rainbow Serpent

Wherever there is water, it is said, the Rainbow Serpent is active. The following provides information on the Rainbow Serpent and its activities, as they are currently understood, in the south-west of Western Australia.

In Aboriginal tradition, the Earth and Spirit are one. Aboriginal belief has been that there is an interconnectedness and interrelatedness permeating all existence ranging through physical and spiritual realms.

> Our [ancestors'] spiritual beliefs are laid in so many million
> ways [including] in each grain of sand.... Each grain of sand
> is Spirit. The Spiritual Belief is in it. That is what we mean
> when we say Grain of Sand, Pebble, Rock, Leaf, Grassroots of
> the Tree, the Wind, the Night, the Day, the Air we breathe.
>   It is said many, many times...the Spiritual Belief is in the
> whole of the land.[36]

The principal Creator-Being, or spiritual ancestor, of the Nyoongar Tribe of south-west Western Australia is conceptualized as an immense winged serpent-like creature, the Rainbow Serpent of the Dreaming, known as the Waugal. It is akin to the great Rainbow Serpent featured in the mythology of the many Aboriginal nations throughout Australia.

[35]Channelled by Edwin Courtenay, London, 16.8.1999.
[36]Excerpt from *Always Was, Always Will Be – The Sacred Grounds of the Waugal* by Martha Ansara.
 Published by Martha Ansara, Canberra, 1989.

UNDER THE BLUE CANOPY

Emergence into union of heaven and earth.
Sandra Hill

The Nyoongar name Waugal apparently comes from the word "Waug", meaning soul, spirit, breath. "The Dreaming" is a continuous process of creation, which began long ago in the period called the Dreamtime, when the physical features of the land were formed by creator spirits who were neither human nor animal, but with attributes of both.

The Waugal is said to have created the landscape of the Nyoongar territories in a wide arc, from the Porongorup Range in the extreme south to the Swan/Canning/Avon River system of what is now the Perth area. Through the actions of this primordial ancestor, river systems, flora, fauna and humanity evolved, and from the Dreamtime, sacred places were formed along the creation path followed by the Rainbow Serpent. This path was known as the Dreaming Track, and is often marked by water -- springs, streams, wetlands.

In the days when Aboriginal traditional practices were intact, this track was an initiation path. It is understood that young males from all the clans of the Nyoongar Tribe came together for tutelage by elders from many specific camps along the Waugal trail, visiting each of approximately 120 camps and eventually returning to their own people after travelling the path for years.

These days, there is a walk trail stretching from the Perth hills to Albany on the south coast, near the Porongorups. This trail is known as the Bibbulmun Track, named after a Nyoongar clan which frequented the Albany area. Although its route does not necessarily follow or encompass the Nyoongars' traditional pathways, our feeling is that it does coincide at certain points. Certainly, as one walks on the track, one can become attuned to the "spirit" of the Bibbulmun who journeyed on foot over long distances to care for and celebrate their land.

In a wider sense, my understanding is that the "spirit" of the land is available to whoever wishes to tread it in unity with Spirit, and in that joyousness rehearsing once again the Creator role. Perhaps, in that mode, the old sacred paths can be honoured and new sacred paths and places can be created.

The following are reports of some of the Holy Grail work that was carried out in Western Australia.

(Lesley)

WEAVERS OF DREAMS

We are the Weavers of Dreams
The Bringers of Truth.

We dance eternally to
The sound of creation.

Joy is our essence
Love is our expression.

Through the magic of Light
We create forms of beauty
Yet unimaginable.

Shanti, Shanti, Shanti, unto all.

(Felicity, London, October 1999)

FIRST ACTIVATION AT MARGARET RIVER

(13.3.1999)

Shortly after the arrival of the Codes in the South-West, I took them to Margaret River to share the Grail *water* with Jill, the only other Australian Grail Knight, who took a short break from her very demanding job to meet. Jill's six- to seven-day-a-week work commitment was to last until June.

The Margaret River region, named for the beautiful river that makes its serene way through the landscape, is an ancient forested area that borders the Indian Ocean between Cape Naturaliste and Cape Leeuwin. The rugged coastline alternates between clear white sandy beaches and majestic rock outcrops which are said to have been part of the Himalayan system long ago. The whole area is one timeless sacred vortex that resonates a quiet knowingness.

My understanding is that in Lemurian times there was a "Light House" in a meadowed area near Cape Naturaliste -- as there is, at the Cape's tip, in a third-dimensional sense these days. But the Lemurian Light House was literally a Centre of Light, designed to generate, hold and radiate Light throughout the region and beyond. One can still feel the effect of that Light in this nurturing area as one treads the land today.

142

It seemed to me that part of the work of the Grail Codes was to renew and reinforce these energies attached to the land.

Within this extensive vortex are particularly strong power places -- often associated with water, typically the haunt of the Creator Rainbow Serpent. One such vortex is in the Margaret River valley near the town of the same name. Another is at Prevelly, the point where the river enters the sea. This latter vortex I was to visit with the Grail Codes on Sakwa Dawa Day, May 30 -- a Buddhist Festival, and a time when every action is said to be magnified 10 million times.

Now, as I drove across the river to leave the town after meeting with Jill, I felt an irresistible pull to stop and walk back to the water. I had not planned an activation for this time, but that was obviously my oversight. I stood on the narrow footbridge and, with a prayer of dedication, poured the Codes into the river. A group of ducks watched with great interest, and promptly dived into the Coded area!

That hot Summer weekend, 6,000 visitors from all over the world had poured into the region for the Leeuwin International Concert. By the next day the Grail *water* would have reached the sea, and all those visitors who had been enticed by the heat to swim in the bays near the river mouth would have been embraced by the Codes.

(Lesley)

ACTIVATION AT ELEPHANT ROCKS AND IN THE KARRI FOREST

(New Moon, 15.5.1999)

I had heard from my sister, Pamela, fellow Lightworker and journeyer with Norma, about a beautiful sacred site close to Albany and the Bibbulmun Track. It is called Elephant Rocks. Pamela had shared a workshop with an Aboriginal Elder in the area.

We made plans to hold a Grail Coding ceremony there, and also in the Karri Forest which lay on our route.

Karri Trees from the State National Park

© Printed through the courtesy of CALM Corporation Relations

144

I drove across country to Manjimup, Pamela's home, and on the New Moon we set off early in a southward direction on our 185-kilometre trek.

Our first priority was to find a quiet place in the forest where we could dedicate ourselves to the day, and this we did in a very peaceful glade by the Warren River. As we spoke aloud Kuthumi's three decrees, with misty rain falling, the sun appeared between the clouds, imparting sparkle to the raindrops on the graceful, weeping branches of the peppermint trees.

We Coded the river and the bole of one of the peppermint trees.

Then we resumed our route southward to "Wattle Block", one of the few remaining areas of our magnificent and unique "old growth" Karri Forest. Despite widespread community disquiet, the government had recently canvassed a new logging policy, which meant that even more of the dwindling old growth Karri could be wood-chipped.

We found a well-cleared track leading from the edge of the road and, the car parked, walked into the forest up a gentle slope, looking for a spot where there were large Karri trees. The bush surrounded us in soft, contemplative tranquillity...radiant greens; vibrant bird calls ringing through the clear air. Timelessness reigned.

We came to a cluster of four or five tall Karris and chose this place for our Encoding. Surrounding ourselves in the energy of the Pentagram, we dedicated this ceremony to all the forests of the South-West, setting our intent as Kuthumi had given it for the "gift" of the Grail Codes -- namely that this gift "hold the Keys to unravelling the secrets that the nine Templar Knights of Jerusalem held for the cosmic forces..., the power to set Ezekiel's wheels in motion, and the frequency for the new creations to come forth on Earth."[37] We released the Codes onto the base of the Karris and into the earth, sending a golden beam of Light through our Third Eyes to the Temple of the Grail. As we concluded the ceremony there was a slight stirring in the stillness of the forest air.

Back in the car and travelling further south we felt very hungry. This higher dimensional work takes a lot of third-dimensional energy! However, there remained many kilometres to cover to Walpole, the next town along the highway after Manjimup.

Finally we reached sustenance and, over our coffee, enquired directions to Elephant Rocks, as this spot is not marked on the maps nor, as Pamela recalled, signposted on the highway. Although we were still a considerable distance from the area, we received an immediate response with clear directions, and so were able to go forth replenished and with confidence! We felt sure our guides were with us.

It was well after midday when we parked the car preparatory to walking the track to Elephant Rocks. Taking the Codes, our lunch and cameras, we followed a slight upward incline. At the top we were greeted with breath-taking views across coastal heathland to the green-blue sea rolling in over smooth, humped rocks -- the Elephant Rocks site of feminine energy. To our left were massive quartz boulders. We looked behind us and there, high on a hill, and etched majestically against the skyline, were stately granite

[37]*Trinity of the Flame Send Golden Light from the Temple of the Grail.*
Transmission received by Dr. Norma Milanovich, Albuquerque, NM, 1997.
Copyright at Athena Leadership Center.

outcrops overseeing the area we were approaching. These guardian rocks, site of masculine energy, are known as the "Pyramid Rocks". There was magnificent balance in the whole area, whose energies were deeply nurturing, serene, ageless and permanent.

Elephant Rocks

More neoliths loomed a little further down the hillside -- large boulders perched and balanced on top of one another, reminiscent of the outcrops we saw on our Grail Quest in southern France.

We walked down the other side of the incline to a reeded soak, and then through a sky-topped tunnel of stillness between towering smooth granite boulders onto the deserted beach. The humped rocks continued from the beach into the waters of the bay as if gentle, stalwart elephants were watching out to sea. A spring of clear, fresh water from the soak meandered peacefully but single-mindedly through the rock passage to deliver itself to the ocean. Waves were washing up to and between the beach rocks as we walked across the soft sands to climb a large, flat boulder. Here we sat to eat our lunch and dangle our feet in the delightfully warm water.

After lunch we walked back across the sand to the two towering rocks which gave passage to the stream, to hold our ceremony. Once again we surrounded ourselves with the energy of the Pentagram, sent a golden beam of Light to the Temple of the Grail and silently recited the Invocation to the Light. Standing in the stream and with our bodies in contact with the rocks, we delivered the Grail Codes into the area.

As we finished Coding we looked across the small elephant-encircled bay. The weather had become blue-skied and sunny for us while we had been there. Now, on the southern horizon, clouds appeared -- all white except for one which was greyish and was in the shape of a flying saucer. We knew we had friends with us.

(Lesley)

ACTIVATION AT ST. JOHN'S BROOK, NANNUP

(Winter Solstice, 22.6.1999)

As the Solstice approached I contacted Jill, who had now resigned from her job, to arrange a joint Grail Coding expedition.

I should not have been surprised to find that, although we had not previously discussed it, we had both been working towards an activation in the same area. Jill had visited Nannup the previous week and had received intuitive information as to its "specialness", while, at the same time, I had been researching the ancient Rainbow Serpent Creation tracks and, although the exact location of some of the tracks was uncertain, had concluded it was fitting to open the way to renewed co-creation for the Millennium in this area. We agreed that the beautiful St. John's Brook, close to Nannup, was an appropriate location.

Early in the morning of Solstice Day Jill and I left Busselton, on the south-west coast, to drive 60 kilometres inland through pastoral and state forest landscapes. Rain had been forecast for later in the day, but soon after our arrival in the small township of Nannup it came down in relentless torrents. There was nothing for it but to adjourn for morning tea while the countryside received a rigorous cleansing! Rain was to characterize most activations from then onwards.

Eventually the weather cleared sufficiently for us to move off to the St. John's Brook National Park.

After the rain the brook was more like a small river, its swift currents making their way over large, smooth rocks on the valley floor. The air was refreshed with eucalyptus fragrance from the wooded valley slopes.

We climbed to the top of the southern slope and from the heights took in the brook's winding course. Having called upon our friends in the Celestial Realms who were present during the Grail Journey -- Kuthumi, El Morya, Joan of Arc, Archangels Michael, Raphael and Zadkiel, Isis, Venus and Sananda -- and formed our intent that the landscape be re-inforced in divine Oneness, we did our first activation here, the site marked by a multi-coloured rock displaying its russet reds, purples and white from the bole of a hollow Marri tree. Then we stood in silent meditation.

Following this, we returned to the water's edge, Jill holding a beautifully rounded water-washed stone found near the foot of the slope. Standing on the shore, we poured the blessed Grail Codes into the water with the intent that they carry the Grail *Wisdom and Oneness* far and wide, thus renewing the land and the life of all that they touched.

Shortly after, Jill found a little pink glitter heart apparently washed up at our activation site!

(Lesley)

147

ENCODING AT ELLENSBROOK, MARGARET RIVER

(18.9.1999)

It was a clear Spring day and this was to be the last of our Code activations in the South-West. Lesley and I had decided on Ellensbrook, a lovely setting we had both used on previous occasions when a special place was needed. It is an historical site -- one of the original settlers' homesteads and surrounding lands. It is close to the coast, with a brook, spring, cave and waterfall, all beautifully connected by paths and bridges under a majestic canopy of trees.

Lesley and I had arranged to meet at the entrance to Ellensbrook homestead, and our friend Jan, who had been a great supporter of our Journeys, joined us. On our arrival the roadway was inaccessible to vehicles, as it was under repair. The time on the car-clock was 11.11. We walked along the road towards the homestead deciding what we should do now, as the 5 kilometres to our chosen location seemed too far to walk. Looking up, I noticed an eagle circling, and, as we watched, it flew off southward. We took this as a sign to head south to a higher section of the Ellensbrook. We climbed into the car; the clock read 12.12. Exactly one hour and one minute had gone by -- perhaps the timing was important?

Arriving at the brook in good time and being able to park only metres from the water afforded easy access to a suitable spot. As the banks were quite steep in this section, we decided to sit on the small wooden bridge that crossed the Ellensbrook. Facing north-west and down-stream, with our legs dangling, we watched the gentle play of Light on the water and the dappled shadows on the grassy area on either side of the brook.

Lesley had prepared some invocations, and those of the Celestial Realms connected with the Journey were invited to join us. They arrived as our meditation commenced. Standing on either bank, they embedded spears of Light into the Earth at their feet. The three of us in turn added our Codes to the stream. Those of the Celestial Realm then added their own Coding to the waters of Ellensbrook -- all in different forms -- crystals, petals or sand that shimmered with colour and Light. Kuthumi, with his usual humour, blew bubbles from a small golden ring dipped into the Holy Grail; these floated down bursting on the brook's surface.

We sat in silence as the Light cut shafts into the water, illuminating all that lay below the surface -- golden Light that seemed to penetrate deep below the stony bed of the stream.

With feelings of gratitude from both realms, our ceremony came to a close.

(Jill)

FINAL CEREMONY - KING'S PARK
- Resting Place of the Rainbow Serpent -

(Spring Equinox, 23.9.1999)

It's Time for Healing - Ourselves and the Land[38]

© Axel Kayser

The last ceremony was planned to be held at the Spring Equinox, centred around Mt. Eliza in King's Park, traditionally believed to be the permanent resting place of the Rainbow Serpent between his Creation Journeys through the waterways of the South-West.

Mt. Eliza is a tall, extended limestone cliff bordering the wide sweep of the Swan River as it meanders westward beyond Perth towards the Indian Ocean. Atop the flattened escarpment is (now) a 440-hectare park composed primarily of preserved bushland together with some lawns and cultivated gardens. According to Aboriginal tradition, it was in this area that the Rainbow Serpent dwelt.

There is a spring at the base of the mount, which used to spread itself across the sparkling white sands to meet the river. This spring marked the point of emergence from the Rainbow Serpent's resting place under the mount, and the whole location was treated with great reverence and considered very sacred by the Aboriginal peoples.

These days, the spring is called Kennedy's Fountain and has been surrounded by stone-work, with what looks like a little shrine at the point where the water emerges from the Earth.

This spring was the location of the first activation.

[38]Quoted from a song composed and sung by Aboriginal artists for National Day of Reconciliation, 1999.

The planned location of the second activation was at the site of another spring part-way down the southern slopes of Mt. Eliza. According to tradition, the Waugal created this water-source, then went underground, emerging at the base of the mount to generate the fresh-water spring at the Kennedy Fountain site. The second spring has become associated with a more recent settlers' creation of ornamental pools and sculpture known as the Pioneer Women's Fountain.

I visited the park a fortnight before the ceremonies to check this second location. Little did I anticipate the turn events would take. To my utter amazement the whole area was fenced off from public access, and the southern slopes where I had thought to find the spring had become a construction site. On the slopes above the Memorial Fountain (still fenced off), preparations were being made for a huge Spring Wildflower Festival.

I was completely non-plussed. What to do?

I began to walk the perimeter of the fencing -- a huge area, which after some time took me to a path bordering the precipitous edge of the cliff. Suddenly the path took a right-angle bend, and just as suddenly events took a completely unexpected turn. There, on the other arm of the bend, were three Aboriginal women walking towards me.

We stopped, greeted each other warmly, and began to talk. I was overjoyed to meet them and immediately knew that this meeting was to show me the direction to take with the Grail ceremonies.

Two of the women sat on the edge of the cliff gazing out over the river while the third woman, G-, and I talked. She was a Nyoongar and was showing the other two, visitors, the "Women's Business" sites in the park. She told me how sacred to the Rainbow Serpent this area is. Our animated conversation must have lasted at least 20 minutes.

We spontaneously embraced at the end and arranged to meet when I returned to Perth for the Grail Code ceremonies. I knew this encounter was the solution to the (apparent) problem of the fenced-off site, although at that stage I did not know how. As I write, I think of the frequent teaching of the Masters: "The solution to every problem/riddle lies within it!"

Driving home, immersed in the good feeling of this wonderful synchronicity, it suddenly occurred to me to invite G- to join the Equinox ceremonies. The ceremonies were to be the culminating acknowledgement of, and contribution to, creation/re-creation in this land, with the final sealing of intent for Reconciliation between the original inhabitants and the later settlers, and movement forward of a united humanity. Up to this point, our activations had carried this intent but there had never been an Aboriginal participant. Although years earlier a group of us had shared a ceremony for the 12:12 portal opening with three Aboriginal Elders at the entrance to a sacred cave at Margaret River, these folk were now advanced in age and would have found onerous the extended driving and walking required for each ceremony. Now another opening to share had been provided.

When G- and I met again, she agreed to take part in the ceremonies.

The arrangements for the activations seemed to need to be very gradual. Whatever was forming needed time. And I needed to secure "official" permission for entrance through the fenced-off site for the second ceremony. The best I could manage was to gain access to the Pioneer Women's Memorial Fountain, but both G- and I felt that this was appropriate. G- said the site was very much a "Women's Business" area, and that in fact the spring I had been seeking was further south.

G- and I finally met on September 23, the day of the Equinox.

In the southern hemisphere, the September Equinox occurs in Spring, the time in Nature when the blueprints laid down in the Winter Solstice are brought forth into manifestation. In these culminating ceremonies at the dwelling place of the Creator Rainbow Serpent, I held the visualization of the Grail Code blueprints, laid down in so many ceremonies throughout the land, now being brought forth into manifestation.

We began our joint work by the spring at the base of Mt. Eliza where we shared our intent of Oneness. We each said a prayer expressing this intent, followed by a silent meditation.

Following this, we each poured some Grail *water* into the spring.

There was a time of sadness at the beginning of this and the next ceremony, with G-'s deeply felt awareness of the lack of inclusion of her People in our society up to this point, and the difficulties they have encountered in participating fully and justly. It was a reminder that the seeds we had sown into manifestation with the Grail Codes work would call from us our conscious nurturing and continuing awareness in order to reinforce their duration.

We continued our ceremony beside the Pioneer Women's Memorial Fountain and lake. Here G- suggested that, instead of each separately pouring the Grail Codes into the water, we should together hold the Codes, one hand over the other, and together place them in the water. It was such a beautiful idea; a tangible feeling of peace enveloped us and the whole area afterwards.

By now it was late in the afternoon, and after we had shared a coffee together my friend had to leave. I went on alone to carry out the third activation at "Success Hill" where the State Parliament stands.

In conclusion...G- told me that in her tradition, ceremonies such as the ones we had just carried out would normally be shared with a whole group of friends...that "sharing" is the key to most Aboriginal practices. We agreed that we would meet again at the same sites, each bringing our friends, to share more widely the intentions we had anchored with our Grail Codes ceremonies.

(Lesley)

PART FIVE

SANCTUARY OF THE DIVINE MOTHER

Our term of 21 months of spiritual work in the countries of England, America and Australia completed, a "Pilgrims' Peace March" takes us to the Holy City of Lourdes.

The Esoteric Mary

A CELEBRATION OF LIGHT

With the completion of our three seven-month Grail Coding cycles in England, America and Australia in sight, Master Kuthumi called for a "Pilgrims' Peace March" to be undertaken at the end of October 1999. He guided a group of 98 Lightworkers from Lisbon, Portugal, via Fatima to Lourdes, France, from where part of the *holy water* that was charged with the Grail Codes had originated. Fifteen of the Grail Knights participated in the "Pilgrims' Peace March".

Our intent throughout our Grail Quest and Grail Coding work has been Oneness -- with the Earth, with our fellow beings, with Spirit; and in Oneness from the Sanctuary of Being, the en-Light-ened Heart-Mind, to co-create with Spirit the perfected world of the Seventh Golden Age -- Heaven on Earth.

At Lourdes our work was to culminate in the anchoring of our intent in the Sanctuary of the Divine Mother on All Saints' Day, 1999. In the Celtic calendar, this was the first day of the New Year. With the dream of the Earth's fifth-dimensional future dedicated at Lourdes and the radiance of the Grail Light ever increasing in the world, it was truly to be a day to take the Earth into a New Era.

Our final ceremony was conducted in the meadows close to the Grotto and the Basilica, surrounded by colourful Autumn tints that sparkled in brilliant warm sunshine under a clear blue sky. In this heart-warming atmosphere, rejoicing with jubilation, the Grail Codes were used for the last time.

As we unite once again, some symbolically, we complete the circle -- the Codes being entrusted to Lourdes on All Saints' Day, 1999.

The rose within our hearts weeps with the sweet dew of victory, for we have now fused the Immaculate Heart of the Divine Mother within the precious Codes, completing our mission.

(Lesley, Gisela, Ruth)

ROSE OF THE HEART

May the Beauty of the Rose
Be expressed through all hearts
Its gentleness enfold in petals of soft grace.

May the Perfume of the Rose
Uplift all into perfect Divine expression
Its colour sing the song of glorious harmony.

May the Essence of the Rose
Bring all into the truth of eternal Love
Its spirit enlighten through pure radiance.

(Felicity, London, September 1999)

BIBLIOGRAPHY

GENISIS - THE FIRST BOOK OF REVELATIONS
        by David Wood
        The Baton Press, Southborough, Tunbridge Wells, Kent TN4 OER, 1985

IN SEARCH OF THE HOLY GRAIL AND THE PRECIOUS BLOOD
        by Ean and Deike Begg
        Published by Thorsons, 1995

THE MYSTERIES OF CHARTRES CATHEDRAL
        by Louis Charpentier
        RILKO Books, 10 Church Street, Steeple Bumpstead, Haverhill,
        Suffolk CB9 7DG, Tel. (01440) 730901

ROSE WINDOWS
        by Painton Cowen
        Thames and Hudson Ltd., London, 1979

THE FRUITS OF THE TREE OF LIFE
        by Omraam Mikhael Aivanhov
        Published by Prosveta S.A. - B.P.12 - 83601 Fréjus Cedex (France), 1990
        Distributors Prosveta, The Doves Nest, Duddleswell, Uckfield,
        East Sussex TN22 3JJ, Tel. (01825) 712988

THE BOOK OF LOVE
        by a Medium. Copyright Valerie Barrow, 1995
        Published by the Diary Company Limited, Hong Kong
        Distributed by Alcheringa Books, POB 925, Bowral, NSW 2576,
        Australia
        Tel. (61) 02-48789304 Fax (61) 02-48789305
        Email: Skumara@hinet.net.au
        Website: http: // www.hinet.net.au/~skumara

ALWAYS WAS, ALWAYS WILL BE - THE SACRED GROUNDS OF THE WAUGAL,
        King's Park, Perth, W.A.,
        by Martha Ansara
        Published by Martha Ansara, Canberra, 1989
        Quoted from Document 4 of 4.5.1988, Letter from Robert Bropho and
        Louise Nettle on behalf of the Fringe Dwellers of the Swan Valley
        to the Rt.Hon. Premier Mr. Peter Dowding

MAGISCH REISEN - FRANKREICH - LAND DER BARDEN UND DRUIDEN
by Gilbert Altenbach / Boune Legrais
Herausgegeben von Wulfing von Rohr
Der Goldmann Verlag 1991

THE GRAIL KINGDOM OF EUROPE
by Peter Dawkins
The Francis Bacon Research Trust, England, 1991

FURTHER READING

THE LIGHT SHALL SET YOU FREE
by Dr. Norma Milanovich and Dr. Shirley McCune
Athena Publishing, Albuquerque, NM 87109-1574, 1996

SACRED JOURNEY TO ATLANTIS
by Dr. Norma J. Milanovich and Jean Meltesen
Athena Publishing, Albuquerque, NM 87109-1574, 1992

THE TREE OF LIFE AND THE HOLY GRAIL
by Sylvia Francke and Thomas Cawthorne
Temple Lodge Publishing, London W6 9QL, 1996

SECRETS OF RENNES LE CHATEAU
by Lionel & Patricia Fanthorpe
Published by Samuel Weiser Inc., Box 612, York Beach,
Maine 03910, 1992

THE SYMBOLIC LANGUAGE OF GEOMETRICAL FIGURES
by Omraam Mikhael Aivanhov
Published by Prosveta S.A. - B.P.12 - 83601 Fréjus Cedex (France), 1988
Distributors Prosveta, The Doves Nest, Duddleswell, Uckfield,
East Sussex TN22 3JJ, Tel. (01825) 712988

MOUNT SHASTA - HOME OF THE ANCIENTS
Edited by Bruce Walton
Health Research, P.O.Box 850, Pomeroy, WA 99347, 1985

LEMURIA - THE LOST CONTINENT OF THE PACIFIC
by Wishar S. Cervé
Published by the Grand Lodge of the English Language Jurisdiction,
AMORC, Inc., 1997

SEDONA STARSEED - A GALACTIC INITIATION
by Raymond Mardyks
Starheart Publications, Sedona, Arizona, 1994

THE WAY OF THE WIZARD
by Deepak Chopra
Published by Rider, 20 Vauxhall Bridge Road, London SW1V 2SA, 1996

LIST OF ARTISTS

Archangel Melchizedek -- Nanette Crist Johnson
The Grail Knight -- Prints and notecards of these images are
The Holy Spirit Dove -- available from:
Master Kuthumi -- The Heritage Products, 314 Laskin Road,
The Esoteric Mary -- Virginia Beach, VA 23451, U.S.A.
Cabala Revealed -- Tel.: (1) 800-862-2923
(Holy Couple) and
Nanette Crist Johnson
The Art Source, 1900 Oldwood Road,
Wilmington, DE 19810, U.S.A.
Tel.: (1) 302-475-4922

Master El Morya -- Armando de Melo, Schleissheimerstrasse 220,
Archangel Gabriel -- 80797 München, Germany.
Master St. Germain -- Tel.: (49) 89-303481
Isis -- FAX: (49) 89-3080646
E-mail: de.Melo.Horus@t-online.de

Holograms Jhadten Jewall - Sacred Spaces,
The City of Light Glastonbury -- P.O.Box 39178, 3695 W 10th Ave.,
The New City of Light London -- Vancouver, B.C.V6R 4P1, Canada.
Seventh Symbol of the Keys -- Tel.: (1) 604-733-3473
and Codes of Ethics and Morality FAX: (1) 604-733-3573
in the City of Light **Camelot** E-mail: sacredspaces@compuserve.com

Mother Earth - She Cries -- Norma MacDonald
c/o Aboriginal Business Development Pty.Ltd.
Perth, Western Australia.

Rainbow Serpent -- Sandra Hill
c/o Aboriginal Business Development Pty.Ltd.
Perth, Western Australia.

Dolphin Gold -- Roger Bishop
Wheelhouse Gallery
3 Riverview
East Looe
Cornwall PL13 1AJ
Tel: (01503) 262328